Volume 2

PERFORMANCE ART: SCRIPTS

G

By the same author

Poetry

Poems 1962-69
Penguin Modern Poets 12 (with Wantling and Jackson)
Objects
Sun Barbs

Fiction

The Case of Isabel and the Bleeding Foetus
Pig
Come Back Sweet Prince
Oscar Christ and the Immaculate Conception
The House Party
The Fox's Lair
Snipe's Spinster
What Happened to Jackson
The Gold Hole
The Patriarchs

Non-Fiction

Bomb Culture
Man not Man
Common Factors and Vulgar Factions
(with R. Carmichael)
King Twist, a portrait of Frank Randle
Performance Art: Memoirs (Vol 1)

EPSOM SCHOOL OF ART & DESIGN
E15553

Volume 2

PERFORMANCE ART: SCRIPTS

by

Jeff Nuttall

JOHN CALDER · LONDON
RIVERRUN PRESS · DALLAS

Performance Art: Scripts first published
in Great Britain, 1979, by
JOHN CALDER (PUBLISHERS) LTD.,
18 Brewer Street,
London W1R 4AS
and
in the U.S.A., 1979, by
RIVERRUN PRESS INC.,
Suite 247, 2800 Ruth Street,
Dallas, Texas 75201

ISBN 0 7145 3712 8 Casebound
ISBN 0 7145 3789 6 Paperback

Library of Congress Cataloging Card No. 79-84759

Typeset in Press Roman by Gilbert Composing Services, Leighton Buzzard
Printed by Robert MacLehose & Co. Ltd, Printers to the University of Glasgow
Bound by Hunter & Foulis, Ltd, Edinburgh

CONTENTS

LIST OF ILLUSTRATIONS

People Show Number One

People Show Number One was performed in the basement of Better Books, London, October 1966.

Performers: Jeff Nuttall
Syd Palmer
John 'Dod' Darling
Laura Gilbert
Mark Long

MARK, JEFF *and* LAURA *are in alcoves behind cupboard screens. Parts of them, a finger,* JEFF'*s belly, a breast, a pair of legs are visible under, over or through the screens.* SYD *is mounted on a dais wearing a basketwork fencing helmet and evening dress.* DOD *is upholstered in pink BVD's with stocking mask. He is wrapped in a chain which hangs from the trapdoor in the ceiling. The audience is admitted. One by one the 'sculptures' start to talk about members of the audience–*'What a stupid hat'–'Fancy her with jeans on'–'What an ugly face'*–etc. etc. until the space is a network of cross conversations.*

MARK *emerges,* SYD *comes slowly to life.*

MARK. What can you do with a frame you're ashamed of?
SYD. Don't make lame excuses.
DOD. My hands are sad.
MARK. What can you do with a body like a beanpole?
SYD. Don't get mean if God read the blueprint wrong.
DOD. At Leningrad a man's toes fell off.
MARK. I could lose myself in the ranks of the emaciated and great.
SYD. You'd stick out like a sore torso.
DOD. I ejaculate sometimes.
MARK. Abraham Lincoln was a lonesome pine.
SYD. Timber!
DOD. And one day I will get dead.
MARK. General De Gaulle is a phallic monolith.
SYD. A right old prick if you ask me.
DOD. My mother used to wash my head.
MARK. Christ was like Blackpool Tower.
SYD. Hossanahs in the ballroom and distant medieval plainsong in the Tudor Cafeteria.
DOD. I put food in my mouth.
MARK. Christ was a beanpole.
SYD. You can't make Christ into a do-it-yourself totem pole.
DOD. Look at my skin.
MARK. Christ was a cadaver walking on the rocks of Gethsemane.
SYD. You can't make Christ into a psychic pnenomenon.
DOD. I itch. *(Proceeds to scratch with gathering urgency throughout the following dialogue.)*
MARK. Christ and Mahomed and Mick Jagger are all thin like me.
SYD. You can't make yourself into a ritual object.
MARK. I just want to fit into some aesthetic slot.

SYD. That's it. You want to fit an image and as you can't you proceed to mythologise your natural image . . .

Improvised dialogue to . . .

SYD. No good, no good. It all comes down to flesh.

DOD *screams, goes berserk scratching. Gradually, ditheringly subsides.*

MARK. Flesh.
SYD. Flesh.
MARK. Skin and that.
SYD. Lumps wrapped round your bones.
MARK. Skin and acne, muscles and middle-aged flesh.
SYD. The visible map of your deterioration.
MARK. The pox and the measles and suntan and the dewy sheen of lovesweat.
SYD. An exhibition of your unintended acts.
MARK. The bundle of pipes and the skeletal cages and cradles. The quaking limbs and the dancing extremities.
SYD. The weapons you use when you put your tongue away.
MARK. The meat and the little thin bags of warm liquid.
SYD. Stuffed in your carpetbag hide.
MARK. Tied and glued onto your framework.
SYD. Ligamented.
MARK. Nothing to do with the self you make.
SYD. Luggage.
MARK. Dogshit plasticene sausagemeat white clay pipe clay white damp malleable pap you could smear or eat.
SYD *(stroking* DOD*'s shoulder).* Your only tangible self.
MARK. Stuff to my fingers. *(They both feel* DOD *who displays stoical pain. Quietly.)* Clay to my fingers . . . *(screaming in* DOD*'s face.)* I MODELLED YOU!
SYD. Silk . . . silk . . .
MARK. Silk . . . I find myself touching another body sometimes–girls and Turkish bath attendants and Boy Scouts and hospital patients Sometimes I've lain with the old . . .

And a touch in a handshake or a cunt or just a finger down a cheek that needs a shave–that's enough to send the dream coursing down my nerves to my mind where I become aware of the certainty of the dream.
DOD *(moaning).* Get your fuckin' hands off me.
MARK. I feel the certainty of walking along the veins like tunnels to the subterranean lakes of blood and pus. I know exactly how to climb along the ligaments of muscle like a snake climbing through reeds
DOD. For fuck's sake pack it up.
SYD. Look just how real is this obsessive crap?

Improvise dialogue between SYD *and* MARK *while* DOD *says* 'That's right. Keep him talking . . .'

MARK. I establish my bivouac in the scummy lanes and byroads and lie in my tent at night listening to the little suckings and gurglings of love and indigestion.

DOD. Oh Christ, he's starting again! He's off again!

MARK. The wet stuff clusters round me like the sticky fronds of seaplants. The other's veins crawl through mine like fornicating earthworms. The acid juices run across my eyes like–like sweet tears. The arabesques of bodywaste trickle trickle across my tongue like hemlock.

DOD. Stop him. Stop him Syd. He's off his fucking head.

MARK. My universe and every human universe is breathing meat and wine . . .

DOD. Piss off! Piss off! For Christ's sake stop!

Silence.

MARK. . . . for ever.

(Silence.)

And then I look.

(Silence.)

I look and focus my eyes.

(DOD*'s and* MARK*'s eyes meet–* DOD *frightened.)*

And I see lumps.

(DOD *smiles eagerly.)*

I see the lump, this lump, this daft lump of silly stuff.

(Silence.)

That's all I see.

SYD. And then there's only one way.

MARK. I just have to explore, that's all.

SYD. Confirm the common wilderness that's shared with your own ramshackle frame.

MARK. Have to look for something my fingers are twitching for.

SYD. The touch in the red darkness.

MARK. The blessing or something like that.

SYD. Yes.

They walk to audience mumbling 'a blessing–something–the blessing please–forgiveness–give me something–touch me–grace upon us'– *fingers trailing lightly across the faces of the audience. Plant 1 in the audience hands out raw sausages. Plant 2 shouts* 'This is Nazi propaganda. This is humanity reduced to mere substance. There is no respect for human dignity here. These people are denying mind. This is open sadism. What's the difference between this play and the Moors murder case? These are sick people. These men are sick like Ian Brady and Neville Heath and Christie . . . ' *till* SYD *and* MARK *return to* DOD *who sits through this, eyes closed, emitting something between a hum and a whine. They tie ropes to his feet and hoist him up.* MARK *produces flick-knife. Slits left thigh, takes out skinned rabbit.*

MARK *(to audience).* That's the stringy wish that none of you stupid sods ever let fly with.

SYD *(slits right thigh and takes out old wet fur and throws it at the audience):* That's the nightmare crotch that only opens to your hand when night comes down on your head like a warm hood.

MARK *(cuts plastic doll from chest).* That's the child your tongue won't buy and your aborted body goes sour for.

SYD *(from chest takes out old newspapers).* That's the story of your lives.

MARK *(slits torso, unravels old rope, backs up aisle trailing it over audience–old undergarments are hanging from it).* These are the trophies, the shed skins the old dreams. The first sad failing flight in the laurel shrubs behind the church hall. These are the left placenta of the little birds of vanity young men think they can race across the roofs of the city like pigeons. These are the silly brave banners of all the lost causes, the Republican Host of sexual wishes. Pluck them. Pick the buggers like fruit. Wrap 'em round your soppy face. Suck 'em. Suck the bloody things dry.

SYD *(snatching a handful of entrails from abdomen–lifting them in glory in both hands–lights dim down to red–a heavy saxophone chord).* This is your courage.
(Silence.)
Your honour.
(Silence.)
Your love of God.
(Silence.)
Your dearest memory.
(Silence.)
Your best ambition.
(Silence.)
Your secret wish.
(Silence.)
Your best friend.
(Silence.)
Your youngest child.
(Silence.)
Your dream.
(Silence.)
Your childhood summer.
(Silence.)
Your forgotten prayer.
(Silence.)
Your favourite song.
(Silence.)
Your mother's whisper.
(Silence.)

Syd Palmer, Mark Long, John 'Dod' Darling in the first *People Show*, Better Books, London–1966
Photo: Graham Keene

Your common kindness.
(Silence.)
Your best wishes.
(Silence.)
Your lover's eager breathing.
(Silence.)
Your human God starved to rags in your cavernous diarrhoeic guts.

DOD *starts to sing/whine. Other two join in.* SYD *hangs up entrails. They lower* DOD *and then stand back half bowing as though to a hero. He puts an arm out to both and they lean and are supported out–singing . . .*

An interval, and then:

SYD. Now–d'you think that was fair? D'you think that was fair comment? Don't you think it was a bit sick–a bit negative? Or maybe you think it's old hat. . .

Discussion with audience with planted hecklers.

MARK. It's all great though, even if it is like in the play.
SYD. What d'you mean–great?
MARK. It's feeling innit? All that blood and mess and failure is what you feel from.
SYD. Feel from?
MARK. Look, in a sense this is just the dark side of the perpetual situation that has its noon as well as its midnight. Walk round to the other side of the human hill and the weather's fine–same hill though.

Heckling increases.

SYD. You mean that the sun really does shine down from everybody's arsehole.
MARK. The sun that lights up your minds is ignited by human sensation. Every tragic wince is the spark that recreates the possibility of glory.

Heckling savage.

SYD. The pain turns into a flame.
MARK. Every internal battlefield laid waste is a bloodshot dawn.
SYD. That shoots your blood up into all the potentials of the increasing light.

Heckling dies off.

MARK. That's how it's got to happen.
SYD. There isn't anything else to do.

MARK. Well, let's piss off and do it then.
SYD. Goodnight ladies and gentlemen.

The People Show punting. Figgis, Day, Long, Nava and Khan
Photo: José Nava

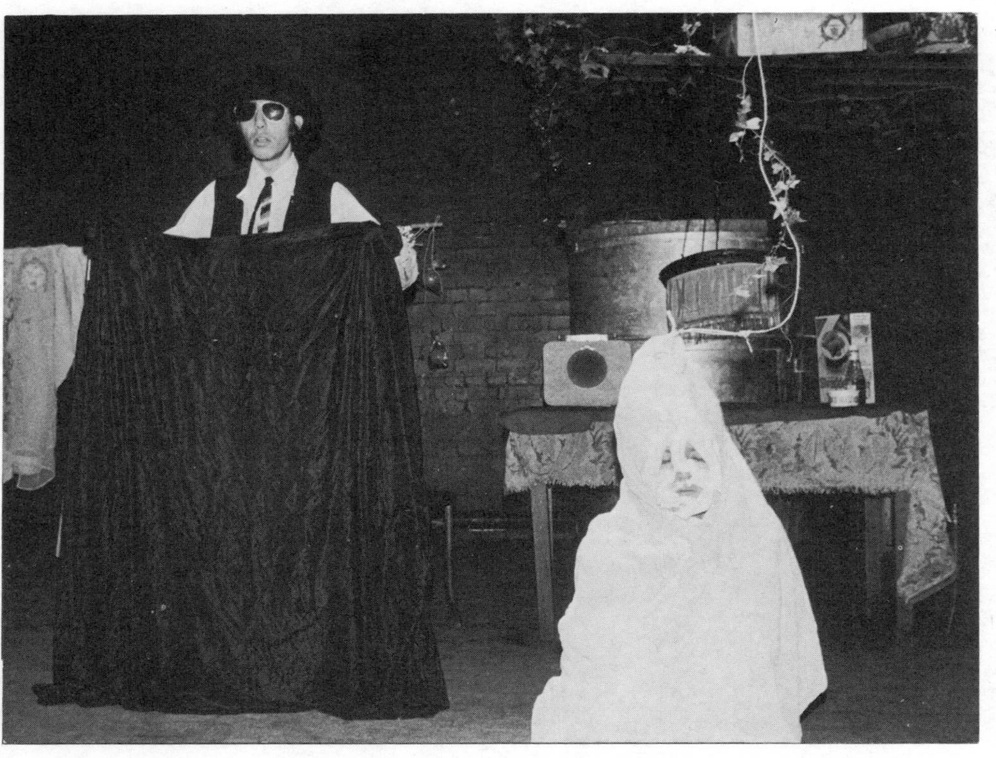

Long and
Gilbert
Photo: José Nava

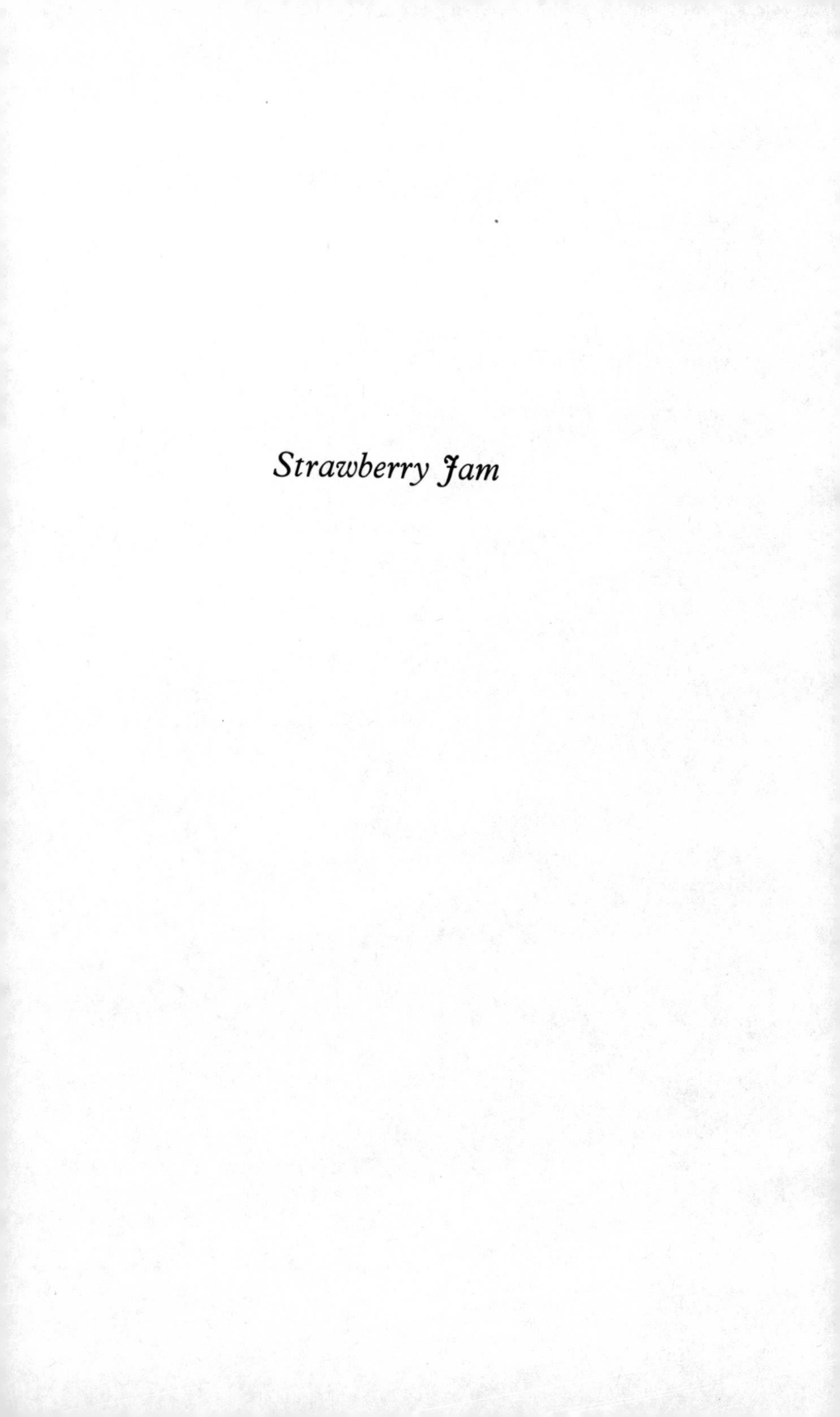

Strawberry Jam

Strawberry Jam was performed in the basement of Better Books, London, January 1967

Performers: Mark Long
Syd Palmer
Laura Gilbert
John 'Dod' Darling

Live music by the Mel Davis Band

Audience enter. Sheets are stretched completely across the basement in three places. Audience have to make their way through three layers to get to the seats which are facing them. Sound of long lugubrious snoring, moans and growls. Between each layer are MARK *and* SYD *crawling on all fours completely covered in old coats. They crawl back and forth joining in the moans, getting stepped over, groping the ankles of people etc. The audience is seated. Sound gets louder, lights out. Snails back-projected onto first (now back) sheet so audience see a dim moving glimmer. While this goes on* MARK *crawls up to sheets separating him from the audience and* without getting up, *just by gathering it in under him, tears it down revealing the image on the sheet a little more clearly. He crawls forward into the audience along seat rows mumbling and touching calves and ankles with his knuckles, perhaps even kissing and sucking at people. Sound stops.* MARK *continues crawling and touching. He must not reply to remarks etc. addressed to him. Five minutes at least of this in silence.* SYD *tears down the next sheet the same way, thus completely revealing snails on the rear sheet which is behind him*

MARK *(still crouched).* I can't remember. I don't remember.

SYD *(still crouched).* You can't. Can't remember a bloody spoon. Nothing to remember with. Too soon.

MARK. Too soon. I wasn't.

SYD. I'm not. *I am not.* I haven't existed.

MARK. God make me.

SYD. Back from the sump. Send an angel over the drains with a string and a bent pin. Catch the pin in my ear. Save me from the blood winds. Back into the body.

MARK. I'll know to begin when I'm gripped in the muscle of a birth convulsion.

SYD. Too late.

MARK. The angel that fishes me out of the sewerage will be a skinny girl in a desolate room. I'm smothered in dirty Kleenex so I can't hear her tears any more.

DOD *(taped voice).* After five minutes, your honour, Constable Jones and I forced an entrance into the defendant's room. Defendant was sprawled in the bed wearing only pyjamas and a fun fur. Lavatory, waste paper basket, wash basin we found to be crammed with blood-stained roses wrapped up in newspaper and Kleenex which we forthwith removed to station laboratories to be analysed. Defendant was observed to be in a state of emotional disorder, that is to say, to wit, crying. When questioned she insisted she had been engaged on this pursuit for some time. Constable Jones and I cleared all ash trays for analysis and removed seven travel sickness tablets from the bathroom cupboard. We ignored further caches of blood-stained roses. After completing our search we thought it proper, taking into account the defendant's unusual manner of dress, to turn in a complete report to the officer of mental health.

All lights out and SYD *screams.*

Two minutes un-interrupted silence.

Then spot on SYD *who has stood, shed his coats and is splattered in blood from head to foot.*

SYD: It was the dark, the living dark, the waters.
It was energy hovering a dove above the vast dark waters and the dove was me.
There was no light but the light that throbbed all sure and white and hot at the back of my own suspended being.
The waters were warm and the universe was a benevolent pressure.
I was embraced by a close and magical everywhere and the universe was touched into symmetry by my presence.
I did nothing but love and that because I was love.
Nothing happened to me but the emanation of love that was me and my whereabouts.
(Screaming at the audience.)

COULDN'T YOU WAIT FOR PIGS' FEEDING TIME?

WERE YOUR SAGGING BELLIES SO VOID YOU COULDN'T LEAVE IT ANOTHER MINUTE?

YOU CAME WITH YOUR PIDDLING SCALPELS AND YOUR SURGICAL SAWS AND YOUR LITTLE LEVERS AND SUCTION PUMPS AND YOU CAME WITH YOUR SPOONS? WHAT'S THAT DRIBBLING DOWN YOUR JOWELS MADAME? DID I TASTE NICE? ARE YOU SATISFIED NOW? DID YOU CHEW THE FATTY BITS AND LEAVE 'EM AT THE SIDE OF THE PLATE? DID YOU PUT ANY OF ME OUT FOR THE CAT? WHEN YOU SHOVELLED THE WASTE OF ME INTO THE DRAIN DID I GURGLE DOWN NICELY? YES YOU CAME WITH YOUR SPOONS AND D'YOU KNOW WHAT IT FELT LIKE CUTTING YOUR SIDE? SHALL I TELL YOU? IT FELT LIKE THE DIVISION OF LOVERS ONE FROM ANOTHER AND IT FELT LIKE THE BOMB'S GOING TO FEEL NEXT WEEK. HOW DO I KNOW? YOU MARK MY WORDS DARLING. LET'S HOPE YOU'VE HAD YOUR FILL. YES LET'S HOPE YOU'VE HAD YOUR FILL OF EVERYTHING BECAUSE NEXT WEEK YOU'RE ALL GOING TO DRIVE BIG MOTHER

GOOSE SPOONS INTO YOUR PALPITATING SIDES AND WORK THE RED MESS OF YOUR OWN LIVES DOWN YOUR OWN PIPING TO THE GLORY OF THE FREE WORLD. *(Pick up and argue with any hecklers at this point.)*

Then, as tape of dream music gets louder, step slowly back to remaining sheet, grab at it and double into foetal position, back to the audience, clutching the sheet in to yourself, pulling it down, revealing LAURA, *prepared rather as* DOD *was prepared in the first show–see drawing.* LAURA *takes a pair of scissors and slowly cuts open her belly. She then takes a number of spoons, all shapes and sizes, scoops strawberry jam out of her belly. Light gets red, changing reds play on audience, as* SYD *carries spoons of jam to the audience and feeds them. Music swells. Rich, nostalgic and romantic and very sweet and sad.*

Interrupted by two detectives, plain clothes, or one detective and one constable.

DETECTIVE *(same voice as the one on the tape).* Keep your seats everybody. Jones, get that girl covered up will you.

JONES *covers* LAURA *with institution blankets and commences to make love to her throughout the ensuing dialogue–should continue to neck till the end of the evening.*

DETECTIVE *(to* SYD). Name. *(Silence.)* Your name please. I should warn you not to be difficult.
SYD. My name's Rose darlin'. What's yours?
DETECTIVE. Rose what?
SYD You can't take my name cos I–don't–exist.
DETECTIVE. I beg your pardon.
SYD. I am unborn.
DETECTIVE. Explain yourself.
SYD. My life to date has been so insignificant it can only be discounted. My real life is about to start.
DETECTIVE *(sarcastically).* Oh really? Do go on. How's that then?
SYD. I was aborted.
DETECTIVE. Oh very tough luck. I thought you looked a bit premature.
SYD. Only one problem,
DETECTIVE. What's that?
SYD. I can't start my real life if I don't exist.
DETECTIVE. You exist alright.
SYD. Wish you could convince me.

DETECTIVE, *enlisting the aid of the audience, attempts to convince* SYD *he exists. Snogging scene continues. Finally* SYD *is convinced. He mimes a rebirth. The* DETECTIVE *is repelled.*

SYD *(gradually focussing on audience).* Will you get out please. Go on and get out. Out you go. I've just been born I want to be alone. Off you go.

SYD *ushers audience off their chairs and out, past* LAURA *and the* CONSTABLE *whose embraces start to get violently passionate as all the audience are urged out.*

A Nice Quiet Night

A Nice Quiet Night was performed at the
Bristol Arts Centre, the basement of Better Books,
London, the Warm-up Café, Edinburgh, and the
Drury Lane Arts Laboratory, throughout 1967.

Performers: Mark Long
Laura Gilbert
Syd Palmer
John 'Dod' Darling

Live music by the Mel Davis Band.

The theatre is dark.
On stage are:

1. *An animal carcase.*
2. *A motorbike.*
3. *A life-sized corpse doll.*
4. SYD *in black mac, shirt, trousers.*
5. LAURA *in school uniform gym slip, lisle stockings, hat, hair in ribbons.*

A spot roams slowly over these to give the effect of somebody looking it over with a gigantic flash lamp. At first LAURA *and* SYD *are stock still and separate,* SYD *smoking (red dot in the darkness)* LAURA *reading* Jackie.

SYD *and* LAURA *slowly start to move round the set stalking one another. Spot does* not *follow them but occasionally reveals them:*

1. *Talking.*
2. *His face buried in her belly.*
3. *She caressing his closed eyes.*

During this section two voices previously recorded and collaged (add music, play separate and simultaneous, swell, fade) come through house loudspeakers:

SYD. Woman don't touch me again, I mean the lot of you, the mums, the black-seam strippers, all you regal hypersensitive sponge constructions of piled up mammary, you grooved clay entities, mud minds, planted people, giggling vegetables. Woman keep your clammy palms away. Don't stroke me after screwing up your tearstained tiny handkerchiefs. Don't kiss me in the railway station in the bathroom at the Monday morning door, up the alley, in the pictures back row in the back seat in the summer grass at my bedside by the fireside breakfast table on the Sussex

LAURA. Why don't the clouds destroy me? Clouds are hammer and anvil. Clouds are elephants' guts. Clouds are dirty old canvas bags of nasty crying. Why don't the clouds gash their nagging guts and drown me? I've been all grazed flesh for the last three years. The clouds are bags of old iron. I can hear the clanging clanging. God and the breaking spring are cracking the iron clouds. I shall graze my skin on the broken surfaces of weather. I am a girl. I am a girl. I am a woman sort of thing. The sky is so indifferent to my woman that I am. Men aren't the sky–there isn't any Sun God, isn't any man in the moon. The man in the moon came down too soon and found his way to

4. *Both of them adorning the dangling corpse doll with flowers.*

cliffs the arabesques of bone. Woman get your grabbing hand off. You mustn't smooth my hair or smack my naked buttocks, lock me round the neck, don't strangle me. Don't fumble at my zip, your breathing faster than your fingers; hold the apple of my head against your rotten melons.

Don't wheedle me again or whine me any more. Don't purr me in the velvet of husk on the telephone. Draw back the milky breakers at your earshell like your water-silk skirts.

Don't talk in clipped tones of the price of eggs while buttoning up your gunsmoke nylons.

Don't laugh in my arms or at my table, giggle as I sit in front of you on the upstairs teatime bus, scream at cold mice, cold hands, or the unlubricated anus.

Don't love me with your mellow legs or Norwich.

Men are funny animals. I don't understand how they bleed. I like to hold them. That makes my woman kind.

If the sky is metal the rain is silver sparks.

If the sky is a dirty old bag of grief the rain is a shade too salty. Send it back to the Devil's kitchen. When it rains you can hear the old bastard clanging about making the early morning teas. The only man left in the sky is a bad-tempered old goat slopping about in a dressing-gown spilling the spells. Clumsy old goat. No God for the witches these days.

I'm a woman thing and one day something special although perhaps not very nice will hammer at my bedroom skylight like a frightened thing and all my body will open into a soundless hymn, all open, all of it. A frightened thing for a woman thing and what can I say but: stand up you silly old man. Stand up it's past break-

arms, don't drown me in the buttocks on your chest, don't lip me with your either end. Keep me dry, yes dry of your emotive fluids.

Woman leave my eye to wander on the cool grey landscape. Leave off your red rags, rainbow silks, your scabs of coloured stone and glass, your diamond tiaras. Shed your peekaboo nylon and your laced gauzes. Wipe your paint off. Let your hair hang dead snakes down. Sacking canvas tweed and rough old calico. Let me look at the clouds.

Leave my nostrils to the wind, wash off your sandalwood, your cinnamon, your fruity Woolworths ash of roses, scour down your earlobes and your cleavage with carbolic. Disinfect your natural bouquets, spray out the dewy caves with Dettol. Come to me with odours of the fast time. It's time you had your photograph taken.

I'm a girl my mother says. I'm fed up to the bloody teeth with scratching my woman self against the broken clouds. Sore from head to foot. Dropping to bits and I'm only a young girl. That's the thing I'm supposed to be.

hospital and drive
me back to the boy-
hood wind.
Don't suck me any
more or speak.
Don't louse me
up with loaded
arguments.
Don't wring my
arm with past
injustices.
Don't wring my
heart with long
gone poems.
Bugger off with
the ghosts of your
abortions.
Let me see you as
a common creature.
Let me strip your
maiden godhead
down.
Let me melt your
icecream pedestal
away.
Foul your forbid-
ding sanctity, piss in
your crystal foun-
tain.
Let me haul you
down and cut you
down.
And let me see
you coldly, sum
you up.
And then for
Christ's sake let
me go.

Motorbike headlight comes on. As lights dim, cut out, engine revs noisily and headlamp plays on the audience. MARK *and* DOD *chase* LAURA *(now in tattered dress) noisily all over theatre as loud-speakers play tape of Hitler war speeches with bird squeaks, animal snarls, and eventually this:*

Nibble the woman flesh–Scissor up purity–Melt pink nibbling purity–girls for dessert–little bags of clitori and peppermints–little bag woman-flesh–girls for the scissors–skin and nipple decorations–nipples and mintoes–skies of seductive child–your smile drunk from an old tin cup–flesh decorations–mint smile–love words hanging from the mantelpieces–pink scissors for the clitoris–an artist with a razor–a lover with a flick-knife–animal dreams for dessert–nibble the purity–girls and drunk and nipples and little wet sweets–wet decorations–lace of your loveable vulva–tin nipples–peppermint love . . .

. . . *with gathering speed going into scream, scream going into whistle, then headlamps out. Continue whistle getting louder in the dark for* three minutes. *Cut.*

All house lights on. LAURA, *half dressed and dishevelled, is hanging (upside down) on a wall. Gives audience time to notice her and then:*

LAURA. I didn't do anything to them. I loved them. Well so bloody what? I love everybody. I didn't do anything, only wanted to pick the flowers. What'd they want to go and do that for? Nobody touches the bloody flowers these days. They won't let you touch the flowers. Look what you've done to me. Look what you've done now. Get within a foot of the maiden flower and it all goes to your head. Well I've got something to tell you lot. It hurts. It's pain. How do you like the look of it? You can't see the fish hooks in my mind but this'll do for the time being. There's a lot you don't know though. There's a bit with the dog and the photographers and wondering where my mother had gone. Have you lot got mothers? Did your mothers go? There was the tape recorder turning in the tiny room and there was the moon over the reservoir. The cold. There was the cold. There was just the cold. Help me. Can't you help me? Cut me down, you said you were going to. You never keep your promises to me.

MARK *and* DOD *enter dressed as a couple of wide-boys.*

MARK. Wait a minute, wait a minute.
DOD. 'ere 'ere, 'ang abaht.
MARK. Why should you–
DOD. You of all people–
MARK. Why should you–
DOD. In this day and age–
MARK. Why should you–
DOD. Sound of body, mind and limb–
MARK. –Go to the aid of a lady of very questionable reputation?
DOD. You should 'ear the tales–
MARK. Do you want me to tell you abaht 'er. You think she's the essence of innocence don't you?
DOD. Innocence? Strike a light!
MARK. You think she's the unsullied snowdrop at the heart of womanhood don't you?
DOD. Snowdrop? Do me a favour!

MARK. Snowdrop? You don't think she's a snowdrop? What do you think then? Why the hell do you want to go to the aid of a girl like that?

–Improvise–

DOD. But we don't swallow that unselfish stuff any more, y'know. This is the Twentieth Century for Christ's sake. We know we're all selfish at heart. So do leave off. Don't be so bleedin' phoney please. You can do without the I'm-a-good-boy feeling. Leave 'er 'ang there.

–Improvise–

MARK. Okay, wind it up.
DOD. No use talking.
MARK. Out to the meat wagon.
DOD. Down to the beach.
MARK. You take the arms.
DOD. You take the feet.
MARK. Don't be messy.
DOD. Keep it neat.

DOD *and* MARK *leave the stage area, cut down* LAURA *and carry her out. Curtains draw on stage. Meat and motorbike have gone. There's a small table with a phone on it.* SYD *is talking into it, laughing– improvisation is okay in this passage but place carefully– the rest must be word perfect or they won't get the implications.*

SYD. No trouble at all–no trouble at all–no–I drove straight home from your place–oh, about three o'clock. What's the time now? What? Well, must get my beauty sleep, you know. What? Yes, marvellous–that sort of silvery colour you get on the water when the moon's just over Tom's Mountain. It's a waste of time when there's no moon. I mean, that's the special magic or whatever they call it. Remember the time in Scotland two years ago? Yes. Well you said at the time, didn't you. What was it like? Like the money the witches left out for the herring shoals. Quite poetic, my dear. Quite poetic. It does more for me than anything, moonlight. You know, I definitely feel that enlargement in the skull. What? Yes, well that's why they called them lunatics in the first place. *(Pause.)* You know when you say things like that I begin to wonder what you see in me. You do? That's okay then. You know just after we'd finished last night, when I was washing my hands at the side of the reservoir you stood there, you know, strongly against the sky and the moonlight on your shoulders and on–on your breasts–was, oh, you know, fabulous. You looked fabulous. I thought Christ what a bird. Sometimes I want to tell the whole world what we've been doing. Why not? They deserve to be.

Anyway they get a special bonus. They see you in your true magnificent light. Okay, magnificent darkness then. The water was terribly cold. Made you want to jump in except that–yes–well, you go swimming next if you want. I'll stick to the other. What? *(Laughs.)* Don't be foul. I thought it was okay last night. Quite a good one. Only one thing–you spoil it when you panic. Of course they won't. Who's to know? This afternoon? Well first I'm going to the station. To dump the case of course. Oh just the tapes and some of the photographs. No, darling. No severed limbs. I'll drive straight on to your place. Can't get it clean? Tried detergent? Oh well, try ammonia. Okay then, milk. Hah ha, goat's milk. What? Well, I thought we'd go to the pictures. Oh give it a rest, mate. Let's cool it for a week at least. We could go to the cartoon cinema, and then on to a bit of supper. That's right, a nice quiet night . . .

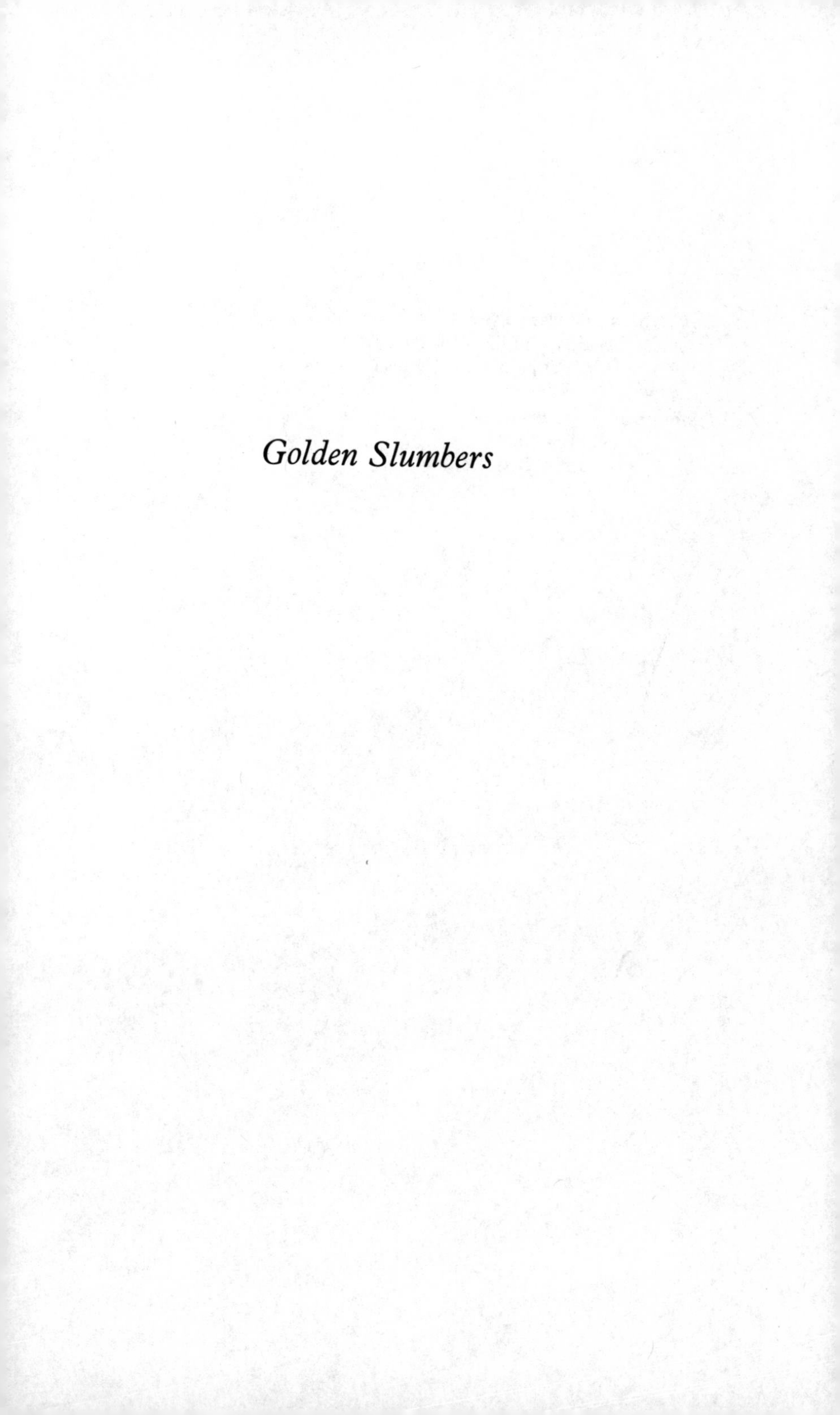

Golden Slumbers

Golden Slumbers was performed in Better Books basement, London, and the Traverse Theatre, Edinburgh, 1967, as part of the Festival.

Performers: Syd Palmer
Mark Long
John 'Dod' Darling
Laura Gilbert
Muriel England

Audience face three overlapping screens covered with child's bedroom wallpaper, bunnies etc. In the centre aisle is a bed. On the bed is SYD *asleep. On tape is an endless sad sweet rendering (solo unaccompanied female voice) of* 'Golden Slumbers' *which the sound technician manipulates throughout the performance–Band could possibly come in with it. Lights dim out to darkness.*

SYD *(as if in sleep).* I am a golden boat. Nobody comes onto a golden boat. You can't come and *you* can't come and *you* can't come.
I am a golden boat because of the golden sea and that's why I'm a golden boat. No pirates. No women on board.
(Silence.)
Bring back the gold.
(Silence.)
Bring back the golden sea.
(Silence.)
Bring it back . . . *(Works this up to a child's night panic.)*
BRING IT BACK. *(Terrified.)* BRING BACK THE GOLD. BRING BACK MY GOLD. IT'S MINE. ALL THIS GOLD IS MINE. YOU CAN'T HAVE IT. BRING IT BACK . . . *(etc)* . . .
(Singing recommences.)
Yes . . . yes . . . I am in the middle of the golden sea. I am the golden galleon.
I'm in the middle of the golden horizon. I am the golden mast.
I am in the middle of the golden sunset. I am the golden pennant.
I am proud and I am valuable

LAURA *(sticks one leg–black fishnet stocking–through middle screen–is otherwise invisible).* I love the silly sod.

SYD. I stand so strong in the golden light. No one can see me.
I stand so brilliant in the dying sunset. No one's allowed to look.
I stand so long. I stand all my life. Nobody can make me fall down.

LAURA *(hip starts to break through the screen).* Goes down like a wet worm at the touch of me lips.

SYD. No one can touch me. I'm all fire.

DOD *(sticking head through screen left–head is painted in opaque primary colours–not too clown-like–get a painter to do it–suggest Hilton.)* Fire? Fire? Is there a war on?

LAURA *(arm and one breast through the screen).* Nothing on at all dear but it does no good with 'im.

SYD. I am the source of all goodness. Nobody can have any.

MARK *(head through screen right. Painted similarly but not the same.)*

Rationing? Rationing? What's this rationing?
DOD. Rational? Mad as a fart.
MARK. Rationing matters of heart?
LAURA. Austerity loving, I tell you boys.
DOD. Sterility fucking? Think of the noise.
MARK. Skeletons on an old tin roof.
DOD. Flak on the Anderson shelter.
LAURA. It would melt 'im.
SYD. I can melt you.
My fire makes you mine.
Everyone other than me is burned to a cinder. I pick up the cinder like an oddly shaped stone. I admire the subtle blending of smoky blues and browns. I turn it in my hand like a jewel. I have made a human being into a jewel. I put it under my pillow and rest my head above it–
LAURA. An' then 'e' as a wank.
DOD and MARK. Oops! Beg yours! *(Withdraw heads.)*
LAURA. 'Ey, they've gone. Can I come and jump in?
SYD. No one comes near.
LAURA. Can I come and touch you up a bit?
SYD. No one can touch.
LAURA. Don't you fancy me one little bit?
SYD. Nobody tastes a single inch of my golden masthead.
LAURA. Golden?
SYD. Glistening.
LAURA. Masthead?
SYD. Regal.
LAURA. High as angels and all majestic?
SYD. Leave me a moment. I'm thick with gold.

Goes through motions of masturbation under bedclothes. Huge breath effects on loudspeakers. At point of climax LAURA *breaks completely through the screen, naked but for black stockings and maybe a bunch of flowers tied to her fanny with a ribbon.*

LAURA. I love you.
SYD. Wha–what?
LAURA. You heard.
SYD. Who are you?
LAURA. Christ listen to 'im. I love you.
SYD. Could you write that down?
LAURA. No. I can show you though.
SYD. Aren't you being a little precipitate?
LAURA. Dunno about that. I feel bloody randy though.
SYD. Well I'm afraid things of that nature–
LAURA. Oh for Christ's sake Syd, give yourself a break. Give me a break. Give everybody a break.
SYD. Take five minutes break.
LAURA. You don't know what love is. You don't know what women

are. You don't know what I am. You don't know what you are.

SYD. I–

LAURA *(sarcastically)* Yes–go on.

SYD. I–

LAURA. Come on Syd. Let's 'ave it.

SYD. I am alone.

LAURA. You're *not* Syd. I *love* you.

SYD. I am alone . . .

LAURA. Love you. D'you know what that means? Love?

SYD. I am alone.

I am absolutely alone, alone, a–*(Suddenly loses temper.)* I'll tell you what love is. Love is a precious thread you lose when you start to think. Love is a wide wide field of utter purity and it doesn't exist–beds and carpets of snow flowers, drift of stars of innocence, original light, embryonic sun, planet of lucid crystals, bruises like a virgin to the fumbling human senses, isn't *there.*

Love's so pure it cuts your hands, it's broken icicles. Your messy fingers get all etched like with tiny needles. Then flex your fingers and the slices fall away. Love's pure as polar air, will freeze your blood, leave you propped in a hospital corner, catatonic as a block of salt. Love is always a long long time ago, is the light that lit the wet dark, was the dawn, and vanished when the dawn turned into morning.

You and your wagging fanny. Your love comes off the production line like a fucking bog roll. Ribbons of pink tissue. Mothersoft motherhugging on the National Health, medicated, disinfected. Just hand in your coupons at the clitoris.

How could you touch love, with your spastic passions? How could anything as human as you know love? Love is never human. Love is what you might have known before you knew you were human. Love is out of reach in the deepest catacombs and the highest temples of light. Love is shaded in the coolest corners of very very ancient places, the first wildflower that all the cockhappy kids knock over as they rush towards the satisfaction of their trivial appetites.

You can't have love and I can't have love. If we lay a concious finger on love love will kill us where we stand. We walk in the dirt my slap-happy little pagan. We walk out of the ether and into the womb and out of the womb and into the bosom and we walk out of the bosom and into the shit and all we can do is wade through until our strength runs out.

Love?

Love?

If the merest ghost of love remains in you keep it to yourself. Keep it locked away. Don't ever lift the lid to peep. For love, my little gazelle, love if it exists at all, can only be a secret.

LAURA. Go on Sydney. Risk a peep.

SYD. What's the good. You don't hear me.

LAURA. Hear what, you nit? What is there to hear? Why listen to a bloke who talks about how lethal love is, but doesn't know that love's so bloody lethal it kills off all the dirt, all your little germs of guilt and baby fear all wriggling about in the sump. Lethal as Jeyes Fluid my dear.

SYD. Makes the world go round, no doubt. Omnia vincit.

LAURA. Omnia wankit? You know that's your real trouble.

SYD. You're not talking about love. You're talking about that smelly glue that runs through the collective mind at East End weddings.

LAURA. You can shut up about East End weddings Sydney. They concern real people and real feelings. A little out of your range dear.

*Improvise up to climax–*DOD *and* MARK *stick their heads through at odd moments with piss-taking remarks which* SYD *and* LAURA *ignore of course.*

MARK. Love is a cinch.
DOD. Into the clinch.
MARK. Mind yer don't pinch.
DOD. Take another inch?
LAURA. I'll take anything and give it back double.
MARK. Mad snake? Pig's ring?
LAURA. Mad snake sounds nice.
DOD. Pigs never ring twice.
LAURA. Once'll do for a girl in my situation.
MARK. Step through the hole. Action stations!

She steps back through the hole. MARK *and* DOD *watch on either side. Big wink at the audience from both and they withdraw. Complete dark. One long slow sweet chorus of* 'Golden Slumbers' *in the dark. Spotlight on* MARK's *head:*

MARK. Night night everybody. Nighty night.

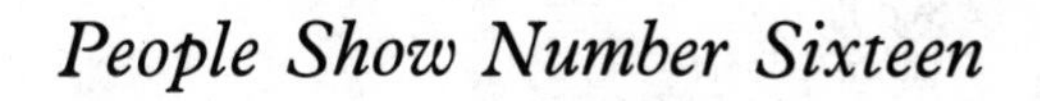

People Show Number Sixteen

People Show Number Sixteen was performed at the Drury Lane Arts Laboratory, August 1967.

Performers: Mark Long
John 'Dod' Darling
Syd Palmer
Laura Gilbert
Muriel England

Basement divided into four cages with corridors between. Cages are big enough to contain say 4 x 4 of chairs. They are made of anything–old display gear, polythene sheeting . . . They should be put together with an eye for strong textures, sacking, newspapers, rags, broken glass. They should be designed as visual environments, masses of texture balanced one against the other–for guide effects see Burri's work with sacking. The floors of the cage are littered with broken glass. Use smells–Dettol, Jeyes Fluid, ether etc. There is a bulb in each cage and bulbs in the corridors. Audience are very solemnly and courteously led to their cages and padlocked in–but really (jailer should perhaps be on hand to release claustrophobics.) When the cages are full (no standing) the remainder of the public are turned away. Lights out. Dim blue flood.

Taped voices, very loud–effect of accidentally recorded conversation:

SYD. And so I tell you he was being sentimental–didn't like that I can tell you–told him it's the only way, the only way if you look at the facts. Deny the figures? Can you do that?
MURIEL. Course you can't. Supply and demand.
SYD. Expanded economy isn't the answer.
MURIEL. Diminish the populace–that might work.
SYD. He couldn't see. I talked all night.
MURIEL. It's bound to come. It's a matter of balance . . .

Fade out sound and blue light to dark.

MARK *and* DOD *go round the cages with flashlights asking for Mrs Meadows–Mrs Meadows wanted for questioning–unlock cages, pick on women, accuse them of being Mrs Meadows, line them up in the corridor. Light goes on over table. One by one* SYD *questions them. He must have quite clear in his mind what Mrs Meadows did and where and how and why and when. Nobody must ever know but* SYD. *Good if a real telephone is handy so people can ring up actual alibis. Use forensic medicine photographs.*

Each woman is returned to a different *cage.*

After last interview total dark again.

Tape of pigs (actual real pigs) plays–get them to squeal and speed up to a frenzy of bestial gibberish. Superimpose saxophone here.

Cell lights on. MARK *and* DOD *press offal and lights through the holes in each cage till cage has at least one wall which is a collage of meat.*

Then LAURA, *with Jazz, comes to Cage one:*

LAURA. You're all the bleak people. You sit on dirty stones and you've all got starving reptiles in your mackintosh pockets.
A mist came down on all the earth and when it lifted you lot all got left behind.
Your only answer to the lovely sunshine is lifting up your nasty noses in starvation.
You're all ready for the drought to dry you up.
When did your women last leave a litter of soft eggs?
When did you look at the sunshine with your eyes open?
Will you come in the sunshine now with me?
It's time for the daylight.

Lets them out, changing coloured lights, different shades of yellow.

LAURA. Come on, follow me.
Look better already. Must be the light.

DOD *and* MARK *mingle with the crowd asking for Mrs Meadows very seriously.*

Cage Two:

LAURA *and* DOD *either side of the cage.* MARK *continues to ask for Mrs Meadows.*

LAURA. What are we going to do with you?
DOD. What are they going to do with themselves?
LAURA. What have they done with themselves already?
DOD. Naughty old them, but awf'ly negligent.
LAURA. Bet they didn't watch where it went.
DOD. Bet they didn't know they were going.
LAURA. Bet they don't know where they're going now.
DOD. Bet they don't know they've arrived.
LAURA. Bet they don't know that outside the cage theirselves are waiting for them.
DOD. Give 'em a break.
LAURA. Out you come then. Out you come. Walk into yourselves. See if you're a good fit. See if the skin's the right size. Out you come. . . okay, this way.

Cage Three:

LAURA. It's sunshine time.
DOD. Breakfast food falling round your ears.
LAURA. Hear the yellow music.
MARK. Sun sun sun.
DOD. Smell the blue colours all round yourselves.
LAURA. Skulls ribs shambleshank shinbones. Watch the light show in your personal cathedral.
DOD. Catheter tube of light. You can all piss your minds at the sky.

Laura Gilbert in *The Cage Show,* Drury Lane Arts Lab, London–1967 *Photo: Graham Keene*

MARK. Sun sun sun.
LAURA. Lie in your own skins out in the light.
MARK *(getting audience to join in).* Sun sun sun.
DOD. Open your reptile eyes for sight.
CHORUS. Sun sun sun.
LAURA. Look at the lovely living flight.
CHORUS. Sun sun sun.
DOD. Your growing higher. Look at your height.
CHORUS. Sun sun sun.
LAURA. Alright alright it's gonna be alright.
CHORUS. Sun sun sun sun sun sun . . . *with jazz to Cage Four.*

Release Cage Four to join procession upstairs and out to the corner of Charing Cross Road.

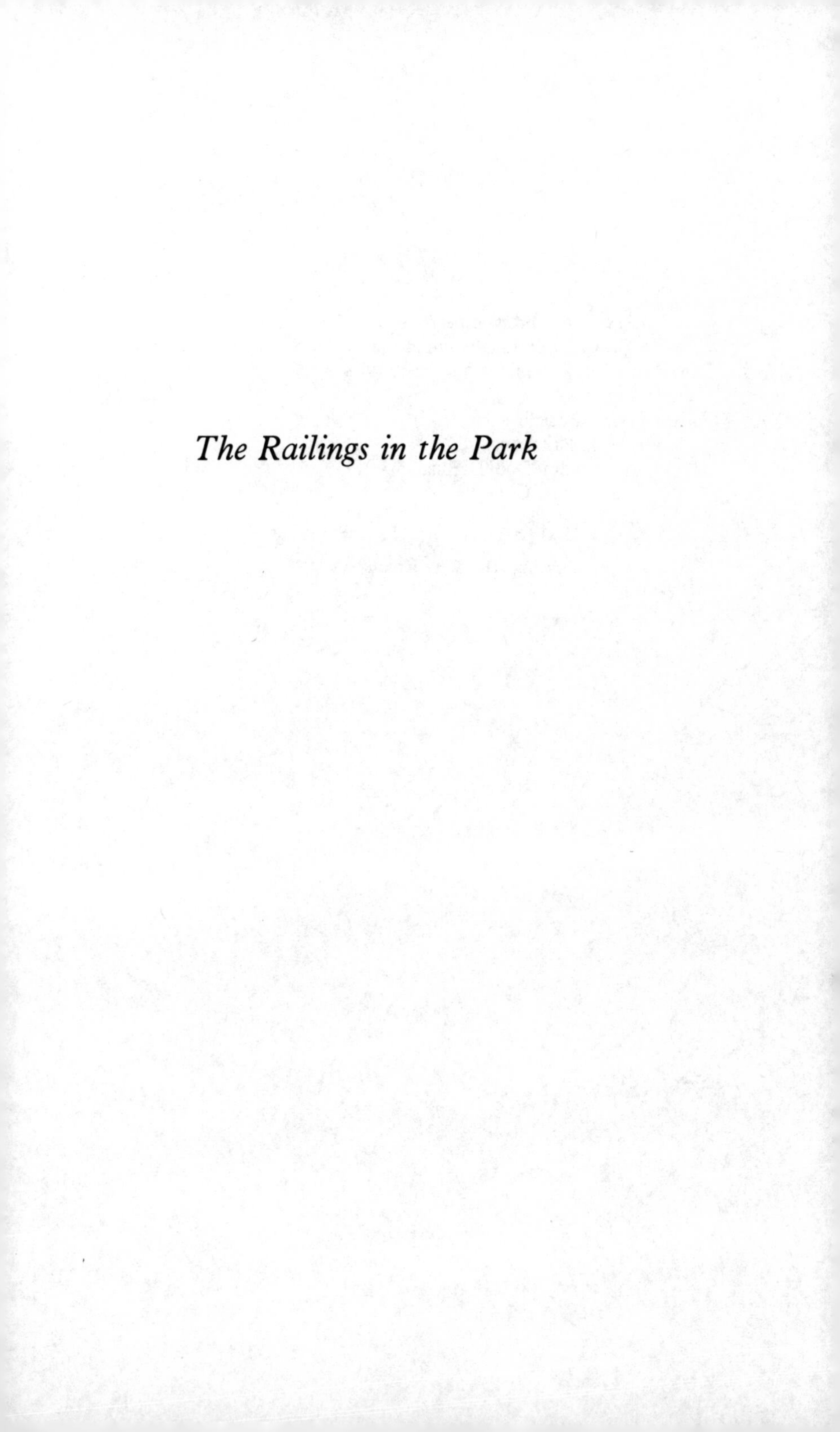

The Railings in the Park

The Railings in the Park was performed at the Traverse Theatre, Edinburgh, and at the Drury Lane Arts Lab., September–October, 1968

Performers: Muriel England
Mark Long
John 'Dod' Darling.
Laura Gilbert
Syd Palmer

Lighting effects by Roland Miller

General instructions and guide lines.

The birth may be humourous but not with a humour that disarms it. Preferably it should be realistic. Recommend that mother and doctor actually arrange with a hospital to attend a birth. Detail is the paramount thing particularly as regards the use of instruments etc. The scene can be done with tights and an artificial cunt rather in the same way that Laura was prepared for Strawberry Jam, *or could be fiddled with blankets and lighting. The doctor should murmur encouragingly and pre-occupiedly throughout the scene and the mother should mumble as though delirious with the mounting pains and gas and air. Their 'echo' dialogue should be carried out in these voices as part of a continuum and, being echo, may begin before* MARK *or* LAURA's *preceding speech has quite terminated. Split second timing is absolutely vital to this dialogue. It should run fast and slick and intense, like Charlie Parker or Itma.*

There should be an intense overhead light over stage area (preferably with an 'institution' green tin shade) and a spotlight for the Lucky Number chair. Apart from that do what you like with lighting. Suggest white/red/white/red strobe effect during DOD's *lightning speech.*

The female parts are interchangeable, that is LAURA *could do* MURIEL's *bit and vice versa.*

Scene One

A wheeled operating table is in the stage area, immediately under overhead light (pool, black cast shadows.)

On it is MURIEL *in the first stages of labour.*

SYD, *in overall and mask and surgeon's cap, walks around, may remove mask, smoke, encourages* MURIEL.

By the table is a smaller wheeled table with bowls of steaming water, forceps, surgical scissors etc.

They murmur to one another inaudibly as the audience enters. They continue to do this for about ten minutes–stirrings, groans, air of slight tension as the doctor waits for child to pass the cervix.

MARK *(in the middle of the audience facing the entrance).* Well what do I have to do?

MURIEL. Castles of steely blue . . .

LAURA *(in the middle of the opposite audience–both are in the dark–the only light is over the operating table).* Stop sucking your thumb. .

MURIEL. Body's a slum. . .

MARK. Is that the lot?

SYD. . . .Fat and hot. . .

LAURA. Well it's a bit grotty.

SYD. Gritty and knotty . . .

MARK. You mean to tell me–

LAURA. Makes your thumb wet.

SYD. Slake the sunset. . .

MARK. That the only reason–

LAURA. Nasty and cold on me nipples.

MURIEL. Whole of me ripples. . .

MARK. –you recommend me for psychiatric treatment–

LAURA. And you should read something besides comics.

MARK. Ah, comics as well.

SYD. Chronic, the smell. . .

LAURA. Korky the bloody Cat.

MARK. But these things don't matter.

MURIEL. Body in tatters. . .

LAURA. Desperate fuckin' Dan.

MARK. No reason to call a man a failure.

MURIEL. Fatal allure. . .

MARK. No reason to say a man's not a man for Christ's sake.

LAURA. Mighty bleedin' Mouse.

MARK. Is that what your idea of my so called impotence is based on?

LAURA. Lord fornicatin' Snooty.

MARK. Sucked thumbs and comic cuts?

LAURA. Cut thumbs and sonic fucks.

MURIEL. Dumb guns and chicken clucks. . .

SYD. Tom Thumb and Donald Duck. . .

MARK. Come on now, be serious.

LAURA. I'm serious okay.

MARK. As long as I stop sucking my thumbs and start reading what–

LAURA. It's the general thing.

SYD. Gaderine ring. . .

MARK. General what sort of thing?

LAURA. You're just not a–not a–well you're just bloody childish.

MARK.*(getting angry).* Oh, so we 'ave to get dignified do we? We 'ave to get all stiff collar and rolled umbrella? We 'ave to get upright?

LAURA. You 'ave to get upright. That's it Mark. Upright. You got it.

MARK. You're a cow.
MURIEL. Now! Now!
LAURA. I don't think so. I just get bloody bored, that's all.
MURIEL. Hear me call. . .
MARK. Twice a week won't do. That not enough?
LAURA. It's not that–it's–I CAN'T STAND WEAKNESS!
MURIEL. Sickness. Bad sand sickness . . .
MARK. You can't help weakness either.
MURIEL. Bleak inside her. . .
LAURA. Help it? Help it? I'd like to murder weakness. I'd like to take every half-grown snivelling man, every limp, defeated coward, every impotent overgrown schoolboy, string him up in a bingo hall and flay the bugger raw.
MARK. Charming. And you'd like to do that to me?
LAURA. Okay okay. Since you ask–yes. Yes I would.
SYD. Feeling it good.
MARK. That's what I have to do to get you to come over here? Put up with that?
SYD. Feeling it fat. . .
LAURA. Oh Jesus Christ. Doesn't it occur to you, don't you just get the merest twinkling of an idea, that I might want you to resist?
SYD. Feel with your fist. . .
MARK. Okay, I'll resist. Anything you say.
SYD. The first day. . .
LAURA. What about you? What do *you* say?
MARK. I love you. Please come back.
MURIEL. No more than a sack. . .
LAURA. Not good enough Korky Kat.
MARK. I'll be faithful. I won't go near her again.
MURIEL. Left out in the rain. . .
LAURA. Nothing to do with it, Biffo the Bear. Did you whine to her too?
MARK. I'll go on a keep-fit course and screw you every night.
MURIEL. Desperate! . . . Tight! . . .
LAURA. Just like that? As a matter of domestic routine. Lord Snooty?
MURIEL. . . .Uproots me. . .
MARK. I need you. Please come back. I'll–I'll comb your hair all night and bathe you in tears.
MURIEL. Razor teeth fears. . .
LAURA. Tears won't clean up the scene Desperate Dan, I want bathing in something stronger.
MURIEL. How much longer? . . .
MARK. I'll drown you.
LAURA. You drown me?
MARK. I'll dissolve you. I'll turn into a sunset of sulphuric acid and dissolve you.

SYD. Evolve anew. . .
LAURA. Don't like sunsets. Make it a sunrise. You're always bloody dyin' on me.
MARK. What a place to die.
SYD. Sow in a sty. . .
LAURA. Don't fancy life as a bit of coffin quilting.
MARK. I don't fancy life.
LAURA. Then I don't fancy you.
MURIEL. Dance in the dew . . .
MARK. It is. It's because of the bird.
LAURA. That mattered once. It doesn't matter now.
MARK. What do you mean, it mattered once?
LAURA. I don't want to talk about it.
MARK. Alright! Block up again! Wrap it up inside. Don't let the air get at it.
MURIEL. Fairly garotted . . .
LAURA. Bloody cold in here . . .
MARK. Do the whole lot. Go on.
LAURA. Draught coming from somewhere . . .
MARK. Sit in an armchair for twelve hours looking at page three of the January *Nova.*
MURIEL. Sanitary clothing.
LAURA. I feel cold.
MARK. Sorry I haven't got the puppy handy. Then you could do the bit with the puppy.
LAURA. Draught from somewhere over there . . .
MARK. No scissors either. Sorry. And the boys are too old now. If you cut up the puppy and smeared its lights over the kids they'd throw 'em back at you.
LAURA. SHUT YOUR BLOODY FACE!
MARK. And your little pentitential ritual would be all fucked up–
LAURA. SHUT UP SHUT UP SHUT UP.
MARK. –And you'd have to think of something else to make you feel guilty–
LAURA. IT WAS YOU? YOU MURDERED THE BABIES.
MARK. –Like maybe walking into the launderette naked from the waist down. . .
SYD. Cornered, cruicified in night town. . .
LAURA. YOU MURDERED THEM AND CUT THEM UP AND YOU DROWNED ME IN THE SUNSET OF BLOOD.
MARK. It was seven o'clock when the waters burst wasn't it, and the light played like soppy violins across the afterbirth. I touched you.
LAURA. Then clean me.
MARK. I want you to touch me.
LAURA. Your hands are red. Red hands.
MARK. She was in the third day of her period. I tried to wash before I came back to you.

LAURA. You left the babies in Barnet Park spiked on the railings.
MARK. I want you.
MURIEL. I can't do it.
SYD. Yes you can. It's not true.
LAURA. I showed you didn't I? I had to give them back their death. DID YOU WANT HER TO HAVE IT?
MARK *(sniggering).* There's only one thing I wanted her to have and I gave it to her.
SYD. Bathe in sugar. . .
LAURA. I wonder.
SYD. The thunder. . .
MARK. You doubt it?
MURIEL. Out with it! Out!
LAURA. I doubt you. You're in doubt completely–edgeless–no clarity.
MARK. For you.
MURIEL. Can't do it!
LAURA. For anybody.
MARK. Sorry love. Not true.
SYD. Faded few. . .
LAURA. Back to her then, go on piss off. Back to the lovenest in the park. Back to the scene of the crime.
SYD. Cream of the slime. . .
MARK. I'm not coming into your stupid dream.
LAURA. I'm not coming into your stupified bed.
MARK. I'm not coming into this fantasy that just because I had an affair with a bird I murdered the boys. Look at 'em now. Strong and healthy.
LAURA. Spiked on the park railings.
MURIEL. Lost in the dark. . . sailing. . .
MARK. And there's only one explanation of your little ritual with the puppy.
LAURA. I'm cold.
MARK. And that is–
LAURA. Isn't there any more heating in here?
MARK. That you were off your fucking–
LAURA. SHUT UP!
MARK. Shut up shut up shut up, like your mind, like your body like what's left of your love. That time I came to see you in the hospital remember?

Improvises recollected visit to mental hospital. LAURA *refuses to remember any of the details.*

LAURA. Laura is not at home.
MURIEL. Not a groan. . .
MARK. Come home Laura. Please come back.
LAURA. Come. . .back. . .All down me back. . .Come. . .
MARK. WELL YOU WOULDN'T TURN ROUND!

LAURA. Why should I budge. Can't expect me to wriggle around like one of your sixteen-year-olds.
MURIEL. Fixed in my furrows. . .
MARK. Laura's not at home.
LAURA. Locked up.
MARK. Shut.
LAURA. No windows. No door. No face.
MARK. Come and kiss me.
LAURA. If they don't do something I'll freeze to death.
MARK. You kissed the children after you. . .
LAURA. You killed them.

Improvise.

MARK. It was a funeral.
SYD. Kiss in a sewer.
LAURA. Freeze to death. Must be a window open.
MARK. It was a funeral what you did. You thought I'd killed them you had to embalm them in puppy scum.
LAURA. Ridiculously cold. Bloody draught. I AM SHUT.
SYD. Open cut.
MARK. Alright. I'll play in your stupid fantasy. It might bring you back home I suppose.
LAURA. No face no face.
MARK. Let's say I've resurrected the children.

Silence.

MARK. Let's imagine that now the affair is terminated and Isabel's pissed off with a technicoloured bureaucrat that the coolness of mind and the abatement of passion has wrought a–*(giggles)*– a new dawn and our bright little babies stand all fresh and flower-like in the pearly fuckin' dew and there is a moist mist of expectancy in the land and we two–*(giggles)*–we two–*(becomes helpless with laughter)*–you and I–we two–*(laughter turns to tears)*–*(cries helplessly).*
LAURA. Go to the park. That's the place for tears.
MURIEL. Grace for my fears. . .
LAURA. That's the grave. Go and cry in the bloody moonlight.
MURIEL. Cry in the blood. . .
MARK. I love you.
LAURA. Are the radiators on?

Silence.

Skinned rabbit is delivered by SYD–*tape of newborn baby crying–wa/breath/wa/breath/wa/breath not the same as ordinary baby crying–* SYD *severs umbilical cord– bicycle inner tubes, old rope, hairy string etc.–holds out rabbit baby to* LAURA *who comes gravely forward and puts a nappy on it and dresses it in baby clothes, then nurses it, crooning.* SYD *walks among the audience* LAURA *has just left trailing the cord behind him so it drags over faces (cord should be vaselined and soaked in Dettol) saying* 'Excuse me, excuse me please. . .'

MARK *stands in the opposite audience and crawls over the shoulders and heads down to the front row, across the floor, weeping, and buries his face in* LAURA's *belly as she nurses.*

MURIEL. And now it's all left me gliding in an amber dream. The hell of it, the gliding, the swimming. . .

SYD *(wandering over the knees of the audience).* Sanctify the riding glimmer.

MURIEL. What good to me now after all the fabulous stress of it, this edgeless evening of soft benevolent colours?

SYD. The season's autumn fingers on our fading mothers.

MURIEL. God-damn the ease, the dying and the rest. I want it raw. I want my muscles working like a beast's. I'll go out again in a raw morning, in the cruel day. I can stand, stand straight as a rock.

SYD. The gateway to pain is locked.

MURIEL *(to audience, getting up).* Look at you, staring, sitting around, gawping at people's problems. Melancholy and muck. Not worth watching. Bugger off. Go on, get out of it. Off you go. Fifteen minutes break. Off you go. Bit of privacy. Come back in fifteen minutes. . . *(Shoos them all out.)*

INTERVAL

Scene Two

LAURA *is sitting alone on a chair–bare feet, quilted dressing gown. She is closed, like a schizophrenic. She sits alone at least ten minutes, possibly more, after the audience has settled. Tape of heartbeats, pulse-beats, tap dripping, and an occasional mad twittering of birds.*

Enter DOD, *walks round her.*

SYD *and* MURIEL *enter from opposite sides, start to sell tickets from ticket books–*'Who's going to get the Lucky Number? Who wants to have a go at breaking through to Laura–make her smile–get some response–anybody get through to Laura?–

Having sold a suitable number of tickets (noting the Lucky Number which they hand to DOD) *they conduct ticket holders one at a time up to* LAURA, *to make their attempts. Don't rush it. If one succeeds forget the Lucky Number. If they all fail* DOD *calls for the holder of the Lucky Number. Lights out. Spot on empty chair.*

DOD. Would you take this seat please? Thank you.

Tape of Mel's group merging/alternating with male voice saying 'I love you, love you, please, please, must have you, you, I love you, olive body thighs wet love you etc. etc.' *while female voice cries. . .*

During this tape:

DOD. Tell me about your birth.
LUCKY NUMBER.
DOD. But the actual incident, do you remember it?
LAURA. Wings are too short. You shrug into the sky with your stubby shoulders, up the wet chimney, out into the song.
DOD. Do you remember perhaps before you were born?
LUCKY NUMBER.
DOD. Many people do you know.
LUCKY NUMBER.
LAURA. Hand in your sex.
Head in your sleep.
Body in the warm.
DOD. Some people feel that when their parents coupled, then, how it was then, how they made love, affects the personality of the child.
LAURA. Bucking on a bed of shattered glass. Mummy's crying.
DOD. I wonder if–you know, somewhere deep in your, deep in your *self*, you feel some sort of itch, some sort of awareness of how it was that time with your parents.

If Lucky Number has left by this time address remaining remarks to audience, moving spot.

LAURA. Dry dry dry as sandpaper.
DOD. No? Well, as I look at you I can make some conjectures you know. I don't want to sound fanciful but there was something of thunder about.
LAURA. Dry dead mid-day sun.
DOD. Forgive me if I sound pretentious but there was something of the crackle of electricity in the sky, in the atmosphere, in your parents' minds, in the very flesh itself.
LAURA. A desert wind and miserable breathing.
DOD. I don't want to sound over-poetic but there was a spark about the occasion–I think, at the risk of sounding over-imaginative, I'd say you were ignited when you were conceived.
LAURA. Desert stones.
DOD. I don't want to sound adolescent as it were, but there was, well, a flaming and a vivid second of unbearable colour. Would it be too irrational to say the whole of nature was, for one split second,

like long forked skeletons of lightning prancing frantic all across a summer sky, the whole of nature, house and town and country, all the spheres were just one moment–

LAURA. The same cracked ceiling always over his left shoulder.

DOD. Just a second–

LAURA. Always the same routine. The same damn silly thankyou kiss afterwards.

DOD. Just a split glass sliver of a second–

LAURA. And then his stupid smug pigstye snores.

DOD. Quivering erect like a majestic penis?

Tape fades out. Silence.

LUCKY NUMBER.

DOD. Wasn't that how it was?

Improvise.

SYD *(in the audience).* Leave him alone!

MURIEL. What's he done to you?

SYD. You come here–

MURIEL. With that nasty leer–

SYD. You get that man–

MURIEL. Should be banned!

SYD. –up there–

MURIEL. A right pair!

SYD. And ask him all those embarassing things.

MURIEL. Cervical caps and wedding rings.

SYD. I mean, what's the idea?

MURIEL. If you ask me he's queer.

SYD. There must be some privacy.

MURIEL. Taking a liberty.

DOD. Well, so what?

MURIEL. So what? This rot?

SYD. This is public you know.

DOD. And a pretty good show.

MURIEL. Downright low.

SYD. I don't know. I think it's embarrassing.

MURIEL. I think it's harassing.

DOD. Not therapeutic?

MURIEL. Think of some new tricks.

SYD. Conning people up there.

MURIEL. Like nits in your hair.

DOD. Man must be bare.

SYD. You see it's unfair.

MURIEL. What about that poor girl there? *(Goes forward to comfort* LAURA.)

SYD. Yes, what about that poor girl?

DOD. D'you think I'm not concerned about the girl?

MURIEL *(arm around* LAURA). A girl needs a young man. No girl can do without a bit of comfort.

SYD *(arguing with* DOD). You did nothing for the girl.

MURIEL. There there my little girlie. . .

DOD. The whole point was to help that girl.

SYD. How help a girl by talking about some other girl?

DOD. Any girl can be helped by another girl's experience.

SYD. That girl?

DOD. Any girl.

SYD. Girl?

DOD. Girl.

SYD. Girl.

DOD. Girl. . . girl. . . lovely. . .

SYD. Girl. . .

DOD. Gentle cunt. . .

Fade down to silence. SYD, DOD *and* MURIEL *are now grouped around* LAURA. *Enter* MARK. *Stands by the door. Their glances swing towards him. He comes slowly down the aisle and they draw back into the shadows (overhead light back on, spot off) as he approaches* LAURA *who at last looks up. They face each other in profile to the audience.* MARK *extends a hand, strokes* LAURA's *cheek as she stands. Very slowly* LAURA *extends a hand to* MARK's *fly. They stand thus. . .*

MURIEL, SYD *and* DOD *(suddenly).* Ah-h-h-a-w-w- *(Big warm sentimental sound.)* Alright, leave 'em to it everybody. Out you go now. I think they can handle it from here ha ha etc. . .

LAURA *and* MARK *stand stock-still, hand on face, hand on prick, as the audience files out.*

The Cultural Re-Orientation of the Working Class

The Cultural Reorientation of the Working Class was performed in the Drury Lane Arts Laboratory, February 1968, and thence on tour.

Performers (variable):		
	Syd Palmer	Bumble Bee
	Muriel England	Mrs Tit
	Laura Gilbert	Wee Tree
	Bryan Williams	Bumble Bee
	Roland Miller	Bumble Bee
	Mark Long	Gungy Dog
	Derek Baker Jeff Nuttall	Themselves
	John 'Dod' Darling	Mr Sly

GUNGY DOG. My tail is under-rated.
Bring on the busses.
WEE TREE. Your tail is under-rated.
Sit in the field.
BUMBLE BEE. Thunder shares depreciate considerably.
GUNGY DOG. My woe is overwrought.
Bring on the railway trains.
WEE TREE. Your woe is overwrought.
Bring in the pudding.
BUMBLE BEE. Thunder shares depreciate considerably.
GUNGY DOG. My glee is hydrochloric.
Bring on the lazy coach.
WEE TREE. Your glee is hydrochloric.
Polish your ear.
BUMBLE BEE. Thunder shares depreciate considerably.
GUNGY DOG. My sorrow is pink.
Bring on the elephant.
WEE TREE. Your sorrow is pink.
Bellow your penny.
BUMBLE BEE. Thunder shares depreciate considerably.
GUNGY DOG. All the world is weeping.
WEE TREE. Lovely girls are leaping.
BUMBLE BEE. Thunder shares depreciate considerably.
GUNGY DOG. My toes are never trim.
Bring on the orange houses.
WEE TREE. Your toes are never trim.
Nibble my tit.
BUMBLE BEE. Thunder shares depreciate considerably.
GUNGY DOG. All the world is fat.
WEE TREE. Sordid pearls for Pat.
BUMBLE BEE. Thunder shares depreciate considerably.
GUNGY DOG. Please bleed my pet with a military crowbar.
WEE TREE. Greasy sweat on the pivot of a snow star.

Theatre floor is divided into big squares of red, blue, yellow, black and white. Audience chairs are in the squares, one to a square, fastened facing in different directions but at right angles, no chairs facing diagonally across the floor GUNGY DOG, WEE TREE *and* BUMBLE BEE *have big painted name boards hanging round their necks. They are dressed in costumes designed by Bryan Williams. They are lovely monsters. Every time* BUMBLE BEE *says his thunder line there is a crash of thunder. At some point at the beginning a firework goes off somewhere.*

GUNGY DOG. Trees have met in rivers of
slow tar.

WEE TREE. Knees are wet on the rivet
of a streetcar.

GUNGY DOG. Flease forget while the
pillowcases flow far.

MR SLY. I was a pillowcase. You didn't
realise that.
All the time I was curled in your fat fuck
I was feathery.
All the time I was sitting in your bad ear
I was all of a tickle.
Little did you suspect that I was more
of a fart of frivolous fluff than a flurry
of farthings or Florida.

MRS TIT crying noisily throughout this speech, opening and closing a large pink umbrella. She has been sitting in the corner all along. How cunning.

Please don't weep with the awful pronouncements.
Far fluff frivolity filtered through funk is a scheme, I assure you,
that's all for the best.
In your vest did the light arise.
In your soggy voluptuous knickers did the gust disguise itself.
Hug me mellow like a jelly or jolly like a rhapsodic disestablished
humbug.
Pillowcases are reported in all the best reception centres. Manly
virtues pursued in the evening of my crease while, let it be
confessed, in the sunrise of your slithery quim I pray for a
plethora of disenfranchised banjos.
Weep to me in the dusk of your throat and I'll bounce for you in
the sunny dispositions.
Sing for me in the noon of your nightie and I'll blow you a
bucket of strawberry sperm.
Do not fear O pretty one,
Pray do not pummel pillows lightly. Never lose the runnels of a
muddywupper gumbler when I plunge a five chord prick in your
evensong fandango.
Many are the days that my mother instinct murdered.
Murdered are the ways that my father figure fucked.
Long bananas are forbidden in the rainy season.
When you make the bad bed don't crush my corners.
See I plunge into the sawdust.
Rusts be thine and all thy troubles bulge.
Farewell.

BUMBLE BEE. Thunder shares depreciate considerably.

GUNGY DOG. Do you love me, Wee Tree?
The ostriches have now arrived.

WEE TREE. I hug you. Hug.
I hug you. Hug.

GUNGY DOG. Will you kiss me, Wee Tree?
The packing case of bananas is in the hall.

WEE TREE. I kiss you. Kiss.
I kiss you. Kiss.
GUNGY DOG. Will you tickle my grumble with a dose of bananajuice?
The lovers wrestle on the back stairs.
WEE TREE. I tickle you. Snick.
I tickle you. Snick.
BUMBLE BEE. Thunder shares depreciate
considerably.
Let there be Bee.

Music–brass band or hymn. WEE TREE *and* GUNGY DOG *do a love dance based on the motions of a gungy dog weeing on a wee tree.* BUMBLE BEE *flies among the audience with his utterly splendid wings. Music comes to a climax. Hallelujah.*

MR SLY *hands out Jehovah's Witness tracts.*

BUMBLE BEE, WEE TREE, GUNGY DOG. Bumble Wee
Gungy Bee
Tree
Tree
Tree
Bumble Wee
Gungy Bee
Tree
Tree
Tree
We are absolutely
certain of the superiority of George.
MR SLY. Many a year since George disgorged
Many a year and more
Many a day since the wavy hay
Dipped fingers in his gore
It's a long long trail to the famous whale
It's a far far way to Jim
It's a long long track up the sailor's back
To the maiden's weeping quim
And the awful din of the firing pin
And the howl of souls in pain
Will make you sick on pussy's prick
Down a leafy country lane
So don't disclose in the ruptured rose
How the miniprickles run
And don't set free in the bubbly sea
The feet of the younger son
For the end of the Empire shoots up smoke
And the army shoots it down
And it's many a week till you take a leak
On the undulating clown
Oh it's many and many and many a month

Wee Tree Gilbert in *The Cultural Reorientation of the Working Class,* Drury Lane Arts Lab, London–1968
Photo: Graham Keene

As the orange busses honk
And it's many and many and many a grope
For the sound of the endless trunk

Sound of marching feet. 'The Road to Mandalay'.

For the elephants march in two by two
And the girls come three by three
And the nasty gore on the restaurant floor
Is adored by Billy and me
And George has gone we know not where
And Billy's in the pie
And we've eaten Jim with the fearful glimmer
Gloaming in his eye
So please don't run or lose your nostril
Sniffing the evening air
I've done I've done with everyone
And the night has made me bare.

BUMBLE BEE, WEE TREE, GUNGY DOG. We are absolutely certain of the superiority of George.

BUMBLE BEE. Thunder shares depreciate considerably.

A small bus has entered. It weaves its way among the audience. BUMBLE BEE, WEE TREE, *and* GUNGY DOG *get in and gently go brum brum beep peep throughout the ensuing drama.*

MRS TIT *(from her seat).* Mr Sly Mr Sly.

MR SLY. I see you're back Mrs Tit. I must say you've got a nerve.

MRS TIT. I had to come back. I walked on the moor with his blood sticky on my hands.

MR SLY. Christ, do you have to describe it to me?

MRS TIT. I had to come, to come and tell you! God how luminous the moon was. It waxed and waned in the distance.
It shrunk and swelled like the body of a lover lost in sleep

Blue light. Wind effect. 'Liebestraum'.

MR SLY. Why, why did you come back?

MRS TIT. Don't you see? You're all I've got.
You're all that matters to me now.
How I wish the stains would vanish from my hands, from my breasts.

MR SLY. Perhaps if the stains vanished you too would . . .

MRS TIT. Admit me. Admit me, for God's sake!
The night has its cold hand in my womb.

MR SLY. Where could I put you? Is there room left in my mind for a woman with your act still lingering in the hush of your kisses?

MRS TIT. Let me kiss you.

They hesitate towards one another, then hurl into one another's arms. Slowly, wildly they dance through the forest of people while the bus follows.

Lights go pink. 'The Merry Widow'.

Long, Darling, England, Gilbert re-orientating the working class, Drury Lane Arts Lab. London–1968 *Photo: Graham Keene*

The Gungy Dog Show with Darling, Miller and Gilbert. Drury Lane Arts Lab London–1968 *Photo: Graham Keene*

GUNGY DOG *(in bus).* Moonlight for God's sake!
WEE TREE. The night has its cold act lingering. in the hush of kisses.
BUMBLE BEE. The stains in my womb lingering . . .
GUNGY DOG. Admit me with a woman for your act.
WEE TREE. I had to come like a lover in sleep.
BUMBLE BEE. See your blood on my luminous moon.
GUNGY DOG. God waxed and waned from my hands . . .
Moonlight has its cold act.
WEE TREE. Lingering in the hush of my womb . . .
BUMBLE BEE. The stains on my luminous God . . .
GUNGY DOG. Kisses woman come.
WEE TREE. I had your blood. I waxed and waned.
BUMBLE BEE. I waxed my lover with kisses.
GUNGY DOG. Moonlight has waned on my lover.
WEE TREE. Stained from my cold come . . .
BUMBLE BEE. God kisses my hands.
GUNGY DOG. Admit God kisses your blood.
WEE TREE. I had to come in the hush of womb . . .
BUMBLE BEE. Woman lingering with a lover . . .
GUNGY DOG. Kisses in my womb . . .
WEE TREE. I had to:
BUMBLE BEE. Come . . .
GUNGY DOG. Kiss God.
WEE TREE. God blood.
BUMBLE BEE. Lingerlight.
GUNGY DOG. Kisswax.
WEE TREE. Kiss . . .
BUMBLE BEE. Thunder shares depreciate considerably. *(Emerges from bus.)*

Lights up—MRS TIT *and* MR. SLY *break away.*

MRS TIT. When . . . when . . . you've done something like that . . . It's a lot to deal with . . .
GUNGY DOG *(emerges).* With deal to lot it's a that it's a that like something done. Wenwen.
MRS TIT. . . . It so shatters everything you've ever lived by. You come away from the scene, of the crime I suppose . . . and you wonder how to act . . .
WEE TREE *(emerges).* Act Two. How wonder you? And suppose I crime the thee of scene. Thee from away. Come you by. You've everything. Everything shatters. Sow it.
MRS TIT. . . . First you can't get out of the memory and the mood of the whole thing. The mood envelops your mind like a placenta. Then you recall the details in a funny detached way and it . . . Then it seems that it was nothing to do with you.
GUNGY DOG. You with do too two. Nothing was it? That seems it then. It and way detached . . . Funny eh? And details? The recall? You then placent an A-like mind. Your envelops mood the

thing whole. The Ov mood. Thee and memory. The Of-Out. Get can't. You first?

MRS TIT. You think 'What am I scared of? What am I ashamed of?' and you feel so cut off from what you know you've done you think you're going mad–And then . . . well, I suppose that's how people do go mad . . . It's not until something connects past with present that you come together in one piece again.

GUNGY DOG. Again peace. One together. Come that present with the past. Connects something till it's not mad. Go, people that suppose well. Then mad going. Think you've done, you know. You cut, feel and sham. 'What scared? Am what?' you think.

MRS TIT. And that piece, that one piece you come back to, is a single crying hunk of panic, helplessness. For the first time so utterly alone.

WEE TREE. Alone utterly. So? So–Time for the first. Helplessness, panic of first crying back to come. You piece. One. That piece. That.

MRS TIT. You make for the first one, the only one, anyone. I came to you Mr Sly. Please don't . . please . . Don't turn me away . . .

Turns to MR SLY*–collapses weeping at his feet clinging to his legs.*

GUNGY DOG. Away. My turn! Don't please. Don't please. Sly mister! You came! Anyone, one only, the one. First thee for make you.

BUMBLE BEE. Thunder shares depreciate considerably.
Howl!

GUNGY DOG. Moons are expected in the advancing breakfast food.
Howl! Howl! Howl!

WEE TREE. Then prevaricate, you ass.
Howl! Howl! Howl!

BUMBLE BEE. Thunder shares depreciate considerably.
Howl!

GUNGY DOG. Bloodstains thoroughly infect my long-discarded socks.
Howl! Howl! Howl!

WEE TREE. Wash them in the waters of the Tiber.
Howl! Howl! Howl!

BUMBLE BEE. Thunder shared depreciate considerably.
Howl!

GUNGY DOG. The waters of guilt are bubble for me.
Howl! Howl! Howl!

WEE TREE. Detergent is a marked improvement on socialist propaganda.
Howl! Howl! Howl!

BUMBLE BEE. Thunder shares depreciate considerably
Howl!

They continue howling desolately as MR SLY *and* MRS TIT *sing* 'Just a Song at Twilight'

MR SLY. Let us to the gas chambers.

GUNGY DOG. Chambers. Tinkle pit. Tin fish.

MR SLY. The long grey queues. The stench of flesh. My family was annihilated at Auschwitz, Hiroshima, Dunkirk, Glencoe (ah remember the haggis of the dead), Armageddon, Mafeking and Aberfan.

GUNGY DOG. Goodness! What relief–the sherbet fountains in the golden depths. Improved detergents.

WEE TREE. Approximately 5000 feet from the top of Ben Nevis to the bottom of the Holy Loch. Softer woollens.

BUMBLE BEE. Thunder shares depreciate considerably.

MR SLY *(to* MRS TIT, *helping her up).* We've still so much to learn. So much to grasp in our floppy moth-like minds.

GUNGY DOG. A candle, my collar for a candle! What colour is mother?

WEE TREE. All the nice girls love a candle.
All the nice girls love a wick.
Because there's something about a candle
That reminds you of a

MR SLY. Prickling at the base of the scalp.
Clammy palms in the small dawns of the generations.
Oh what is to come of us?

BUMBLE BEE, WEE TREE, GUNGY DOG.
Come Come Come

MR SLY. When we drown our passions in

BUMBLE BEE, WEE TREE, GUNGY DOG.
Rum Rum Rum *Thunder effect.*

MR SLY. And the awful thunderstorms

BUMBLE BEE, WEE TREE, GUNGY DOG.
Come Come Come

MR SLY. And the mind is a nasty old

BUMBLE BEE, WEE TREE, GUNGY DOG.
Slum Slum Slum

MR SLY. And the angel of death cut his

BUMBLE BEE, WEE TREE, GUNGY DOG
Thumb Thumb Thumb

MR SLY. And you hear death beating the

BUMBLE BEE, WEE TREE, GUNGY DOG.
Drum Drum Drum

MR SLY. Where shall we wander in the chasms of the tangerine monopoly?

WEE TREE, GUNGY DOG, BUMBLE BEE.
Come
Rum
Come
Slum
Thumb
Drum

Come	Come	Come
Rum	Rum	Rum
Come	Come	Come
Slum	Slum	Slum
Thumb	Thumb	Thumb
Drum	Drum	Drum

MR SLY *and* MRS TIT *stand, a tragic couple valiant in the face of dread, while* GUNGY DOG, WEE TREE and BUMBLE BEE *execute a jitterbug dance round them to the sound of Benny Goodman's* 'Sing, Sing Sing' *with extended drum solo by Gene Krupa.*

MRS TIT. He lay so cold. I could scarcely touch his face. I felt my fingers might stick to his face like fingers sticking to ice. I felt I might leave tiny morsels of my fingertips attached to his dead face and, though red as poppies, they would not be like flowers. I walked to all the parts of the room and touched them instead of touching him. To make of them, the curtains, the walls, the furnishings, some substitute less cold than his face, less forbidding in the intensity of death, to touch something warmer and yet part of him as he now is.

The green of his face, not the translucent green of undersea cathedrals but the thick opaque green of the North Sea on a winter afternoon, of gobs of phlegm left perfect in the gutter by passing old men, old men also dying.

MR SLY. Ah what is to come of us all?

BUMBLE BEE. Thunder shares depreciate considerably.

Everybody howls and the howls descend to silence–Everybody sits dilapidated. WEE TREE *takes a recorder and plays a simple tune through.* GUNGY DOG *takes out a tin whistle and joins in second time through.* BUMBLE BEE *takes out kazoo and joins in third time through. They continue playing, taking audience hands and leading them in and out of the chairs. As the line passes* MRS TIT *and* MR SLY *take people out of the chairs and dress them out of a huge dress-up box. Music gets faster. Light effects in blue, yellow, red. Simultaneous records of Beethoven's* 'Pastoral' *and Bunk Johnson's* 'The Saints'. *Police whistle. Silence. Everybody is arrested.*

The Beach Ball Show

The Beach Ball Show was performed on tour throughout 1968-9

Performers: Mark Long
Laura Gilbert
Roland Miller

Coloured beach balls everywhere, big rubber ones. Circus music. Suddenly silence as MARK *emerges from the milling audience. He is a cushion.*

MARK. Laura.
LAURA *(offstage).* Coming ducky!
MARK. Laura!
LAURA. Coming ducky.
MARK. Laura!
LAURA. Coming ducky.

Extend this on appropriate nights.

MARK, *singing mightily, throws himself and several balls at the audience. The idea is to precipitate a ball-battle with the audience.*

MARK *(back in the centre after the battle).* Laura!
LAURA. Fried house.
MARK. Laura!
LAURA. One way signals.
MARK. Laura!
LAURA. Technicolour cud.
MARK. Cud? Did you say cud? Laura, did you say cud?

Silence relieved by birdsong and a distant cry of utter triumph.

MARK. Laura, did you say cud?
LAURA *(very loudly).* MA–A–A–ARK!!!
MARK. I can hear you my dear.
LAURA. MA–A–A–ARK!
MARK. I can nose you my rose.
LAURA. Mark!
MARK. I can taste you my waste.
LAURA. Mark!
MARK. But my eyes my dear, my eyes my dear, my eyes my dear. I cannot unfortunately see you, my affectionate piglet.
LAURA. Fuck ya then.

A dirty old fish thrown from afar falls at MARK*'s feet.* MARK *circles it on all fours suspiciously. Then he gingerly picks it up, places it in a small shoe he happens to have and gives it to a lady in the front row.*

MARK. I remain in a state of uncertainty with regard to your whereabouts.
LAURA. Up yer 'ole then.

A dirty old shoe thrown from afar falls at MARK's *feet.* MARK *circles it on all fours suspiciously. Then he gingerly picks it up, produces a dirty old fish he happens to have, places it in the shoe and gives it to a lady on the front row.*

MARK. My ocular approach to the determination of your precise geographical location is obstructed.
LAURA. Go suck your ear.

A dirty old sack falls at MARK's *feet. He gets into it and attempts to sit on the knees of the lady on the front row–head in the sack–With reasonably sophisticated audience this could turn into a snogging session through the sacking. While this is going on* LAURA *finally appears. She is dressed in a sumptuous evening dress complete with a perfect make-up job and jewelry. Her costume should contrast magnificently with the dialogue that's gone before.*

LAURA. It's difficult to tell sometimes if he's human.
When I found him he was hairless and honourable.
When you look at him now he's a ball of shag.
Don't touch him my dear, without disinfectant, without a protective coating of the old rat poison you might find his mind leaking its way through your pancake make-up.
It's difficult to tell if he's still alive or whether the worms that inhabit the dead are moving his flesh to the answering odours from your own internal rot.
We've been intimate for years.
Crawling about in the dark dank places under the sink.
It's difficult to tell if you're still the same person.
After a touch of his cold dry lips, after the last pale wash of sunlight fades from the corner of the kitchen.
Don't you touch him dear without your rubber gloves on.
Don't come near him without a gush from the flit gun.
Don't go close without a vapour trail and thick mist.

When I found him I took him home.
I hung colours in his curls and small blue flowers round his hard horn.
I washed him with kisses and dried him with slow and muscular hands.
I hung a sumptuous rug about his alabaster body.
I hung a chain of beautiful ideas at his right wrist.
Don't think he didn't have the goods at that time dearie.
Don't think that I hadn't brought the goods home to my own door just for once.
Don't forget–I can't forget–I woke up one morning and the beast was glinting from his sleeping lip,
An ancient crudity was snoring on his morning breath.
Some dead dream had come into his loving in the hour that doesn't happen somewhere past the night.

Laura. *Photo: José Nava*

Don't forget that when he woke his words were brown and his body was gone rough.
Don't forget to wash well when you leave.
Don't forget to wash your mind. Don't forget to swill his image from your memory. Forget.
Remember to forget.

MARK *(emerging).* Blimey don't she go on?

They improvise. During the improvisation the loudspeaker plays a march, a sentimental ballad, Wagner and Englebert and any more you care to add. Every time the record changes the characters change. The last record should finish with them throwing the balls around. Then silence and single spot as they gravely and completely undress one another.

Lights out. Wind. Distant voices calling from obscure horizons, odours, burning heather, damp plaster. LAURA, *in a tattered dress, runs among them, hides behind them, cackles softly in their ears. . . Overhead light on* MARK *and* ROLAND. *Clink of glasses, bar-room conversation. . .*

MARK. Oh I say, rather a plunger what. Right up the old snoodle, thrashed about like a bloody road-casualty. Had a crack at it, old man?

ROLAND. Back seat of the old Aston. Backed onto the prong like a dillywud. Throgged her about, clapped a snide in her ear, threw her out of the split and flat.

MARK. Stab it?

ROLAND. Oh nonono, not exactly. Bit of a prong, spot of the old slime about, donchaknow.

MARK. Willing I suppose?

ROLAND. Positively froddick, old boy. Positively froddick.

Lights down to snody red. ROLAND *and* MARK *transform. They crouch and whimper.* MARK *intermittently screams.* LAURA *emerges from behind the nearest vicar. She is laughing her ridiculing ha-ha-ha. The weeping wind passes again through the theatre. Crouch-legged like a threatening ape she approaches the two men and stalks around them until they huddle together. This whole operation works up to a climax of tension when the pose of all three freezes into a tableau.*

On tape:

ROLAND. Went a bit dippy.

MARK. Can't rely on 'em.

ROLAND. Plugging away like billy-ho in the shrubberies behind the Las Vegas Country Club, suddenly grogged about all over the driveway.

MARK. Well, what d'you expect old man?

ROLAND. Snores around her spotty anklestraps, shackled old boy, shackled. Staggering about in the sled crogging like a ruptured band-saw.
MARK. And what, what, wh-wh-what did you do old man?
ROLAND. Slugged her.

LAURA *claws off her drawers and whips them.*

ROLAND. Back of the car.

She lashes them again.

ROLAND. Glut all over the grass virgin.

She strikes again.

ROLAND. Took half a dozen Johnny Hawkers to ring down her wimple.

LAURA *screams as the two men climb slowly up her legs. Sound of barrel organ played very fast. Train whistle.*

Once upright MARK *and* ROLAND *regain their jauntiness and go to chat up the audience*–'Fancy a spot of the old, y'know?' 'How d'you get on with the secretary then?' 'Get yer 'ole alright did yer?'– *During this* LAURA *comes through very loud on echo tape with lonely Figgis trumpet.*

LAURA. I thought he looked handsome.
I collected a bunch of mountain shellfish for him.
I gave him a model of a child's ear.
I looked at my palm and a little well of luminous scum sprang up.
I blessed his eyes with the running stone.
I thought he looked sad.
I made flowers of coloured rags and sweetmeats.
I hung myself with wet ribbons and warped my body in tattered chiffon.
I danced around him.
He danced in me.
He danced his wellspring of scum in the quick of my personal oyster.
I thought he looked tired.
I made a fire in his aresehole mystery.
I stoked my pet devils all around his breathing eyes.
I sent the small and coloured lights fucking daisy-chains along his blood.
I thought he looked love.
All he looked was a lilac suddenly dissolved and running down the night.
All he meant was the edge of his hand across my fine glass bells.
All he gave me was the hard gravel in my mouth.
The cold stars burned out my bruises.

MARK. I say, I say, I say.
ROLAND. Ye, my good man.
MARK. My old lady likes it in her ear.
ROLAND. Likes it in her ear? How d'you know?
MARK. Every time I try to stick it in her mouth she turns her head.
ROLAND. Kick her bibbies in old man, the only answer.
MARK. Did you k-k-kick in the bibbies of the summertime slag?
ROLAND. Slugged her dugs old man.
MARK. Plugged her babybin?
ROLAND. Kicked her biscuit.
MARK. Chopped her carrots?
ROLAND. Hammer blow smack behind the pearly lug.
MARK. Where did she go?
ROLAND. Off into the evening sky old man, off into the evening sky.

Sudden spot on LAURA.

MARK. Who's she?
ROLAND. Priscilla Plate.
MARK. Not so tasty. Who's she really though?
ROLAND. Olive Orifice.
MARK. Not so deep. No, though. Tell us.
ROLAND. Linda Lips.
MARK. Not so wet. Come on Rolly.
ROLAND. Vera Vagina.
MARK. Bit too dark. Show us again.
ROLAND. Mary Hairy.
MARK. Bit shaggy. . .
LAURA. I'm Katy Queen.
ROLAND & MARK. Polish your bonce, lidy?
LAURA. I'm Ethel the Empress.
ROLAND & MARK. Milk your elephant, Madame?
LAURA. I'm Ruby the Ruler.
ROLAND & MARK. Give yer twelve inches, lidy.
LAURA. I'm Miranda the Mistress.
ROLAND & MARK. Watcha gotta do for a touch of the other?
LAURA. On your knees.

Slowly she wills them onto their knees again. Lights and organ sounds change the atmosphere to ecclesiastical. LAURA *hands out hymn books. She calls out the number and, while* ROLAND *and* MARK *lead the singing, she takes off her shift, nothing underneath, and slowly puts on black lace underwear, black nylons and evening dress so that on the last note of the hymn she stands like a kind of altar figure. She gestures* ROLAND *and* MARK *to their feet and they move to either side of her. Sound of wind. . .*

ROLAND. Incense.
LAURA. Scent.
MARK. Incest.

Wind. . .

ROLAND. Clerestory.
LAURA. Clarity.
MARK. History.

Wind. . .

ROLAND. Mystery.
LAURA. Hysteria.
MARK. Misery.

Wind. . .

ROLAND. Darkness.
LAURA. Harness.
MARK. Hark.

Organ tape starts, very grave and weird.

ROLAND. Long slow nylons of the living God.
LAURA. Long slow smiles of the evil sod.
MARK. Small slow snails in the winter mud.
ROLAND. It's darkness time.
LAURA. It's darkness time.
MARK. It's darkness time.

Together they hum a lullaby, then whisper 'Goodnight' *and kiss audience gently as they go out.*

Tennis

Tennis was performed on tour throughout
1968-9.

Performers: Mark Long
Roland Miller
Laura Gilbert

Enter ROLAND *in tennis shorts and tee-shirt, carrying racquet. He swipes and bounces coloured balls (tennis) around the theatre while he takes off one tee-shirt after another.*

On the first there is a picture of J.F. Kennedy.
On the second there is a picture of a screaming soldier.
On the third there is a picture of Robert Kennedy.
On the fourth there is a picture of Malcolm X.
On the fifth there is a picture of a burning Buddhist monk.
On the sixth there is a large drawing of a penis.
On the seventh is a large drawing of a cunt.

His torso, when revealed, is painted in blocks of black, white and red, yellow and blue which cut across anatomical outlines and divisions.

Tape which has been playing crowd noises, march music and applause, suddenly stops.

ROLAND *circles the audience snarling softly. He should give the effect of being on the verge of a fit. Suddenly he leaps on a chair.*

ROLAND. Alright. Who's for fucking tennis then?
MARK, LAURA *(from the audience).* Tennis, tennis? What does he mean, tennis? Who's tennis? etc. etc.

They bombard ROLAND *with coloured tennis balls. Silence.*

ROLAND. Alright. Who's for fucking tennis then?

MARK, LAURA. Bastards? Get up you bastards? Tennis bastards? etc. etc.

More tennis balls.

ROLAND. I know you lot. I know you lot on the tennis courts.
One backhander and you stagger back into the umpire's lemonade.
Not a man amongst you who's handled a real racquet.
Not a man or woman among you knows how to twang a catgut.
It's all falling down I tell you.
The days of the great sets are over.
Has anyone here ever bounced a ball in frilly knickers?
Has anybody here ever sat in an English summer afternoon in an English garden, with an English summer hat across their English knees watching English tennis played with English balls?
MARK. English balls to you too mate. *(Throws one tennis ball.)*
ROLAND. Well, has anyone? *(pause.)* Fucking wogs!

LAURA *and* MARK *come strutting down the aisle—black faces, big bow ties, big white lips, striped trousers, black wrists and white gloves. Banjo accompaniment.*

MARK, LAURA *(to the tune of* 'Casey Jones').

Rastus and Lucy were a tennis team.
Dey played a game ob doubles wid society's cream.
When one day Rastus sez to Lucy his love
We gonna play tennis in de hebbens above.

Dey played tennis wid St Peter and de hand ob fate.
Dey bounced dem rubber balls off de Pearly Gate.
De forehand drive ob Gabriel was a terrible gas.
Dey made de angels cut down de celestial grass.

Rastus and Lucy! de angel host roared.
All ober de court de spectators soared.
It was plain to see dat eb'ry time de visitors scored
Dey'd got a faster wrist dan de hand ob de Lord.

ROLAND *has taken out a folding stool and is sitting on it, suddenly the langourous colonial (Rhodesian accent?).*

ROLAND. I say, I say boy. Bring me a long cool drink.

MARK *and* LAURA *unroll a long canvas Lager advertisement and tie him up in it.*

ROLAND *(tied up on the ground).* I say, boy. Could you re-arrange this damned mosquito net.
LAURA *(strangles him).*
ROLAND. I say boy. What about a spot of artificial respiration?

MARK *produces huge bellows, sticks nozzle up* ROLAND's *arse and blows him up.*

ROLAND. I say boy, what about the kiss of life?

MARK *and* LAURA *stalk one another round and over* ROLAND's *bound body. Slowly they do a big sucky kiss. Sound effect of balloon slowly being let down. While this is going on* ROLAND *starts to get up but is unable to because* MARK *and* LAURA *are kissing over his head.*

ROLAND. Grad rot your flungle bled.
Skrattle your guzzard.
Skuttle your blizzard.
Flow fluk yourselves and slap your goolies round your gumboil.
Grakl Grakl Grakl.

MARK. Wh–wh–whut is he talkin' about Lucy?
LAURA. Fucked if I know.

They start to walk round ROLAND *who is gradually freeing himself.*

MARK. Is he a larrupped lizard or a horny whelp?
LAURA. Nar, I don't reckon.
MARK. Is he a slow toad or a Henry Spencer?

Mark. *Photo: José Nava*

LAURA *(in the same tone as* 'Fucked if I know'). Suckta pigtoe.
MARK. Is he large George or a hairy turd? Does he wulk fringle or wamble jam perchance?
ROLAND. I play fucking tennis.
LAURA. Snarl a bone beckon.
MARK. He plays what?
LAURA. Snikta slugtoe.
MARK *(pushing* ROLAND *to* LAURA). Do you think he *(pause)* slags rattlesnakes?
LAURA *(pushing him back).* Oh yes.
MARK *(pushing).* Did–did he ever slag a rattletoe for you?
LAURA. YES! *(Pushes).*
MARK *(pushing).* Did–did he sleep weep on your wiptoe and slag your rattletrap all night long?
LAURA. YES! *(Pushes).*
MARK *(pushing).* Did–he slipperslopper plop on your plittle wheenie and lip up the leavings before he slagged your rattletrap in the early dew?
LAURA *(pushing).* YES!
MARK *(turning away).* What a cunt.
ROLAND *(struggling free at last).* By God yes!
By heavens yes!
What a jolly marvellous, I mean utterly stupendous, well I mean really super whizzo, I mean WHAT a cunt! First there was the size. I could stand in the distance–
LAURA, MARK. Yes?
ROLAND. And leap *(he leaps.)* and swim for hours *(he swims for hours.* LAURA *and* MARK *follow him with coloured water sprays)* up the golden rivers of the interior–
MARK, LAURA. Yes yes?
ROLAND. As I stand on a cervical pinnacle–*(stands on audience member)*
I can view at a glance the untold natural resources of the Upper Wombat.
LAURA, MARK. Yes bwana, yes bwana, yes bwana.
ROLAND. Line up you trusty, loveable, innocent black scum.

LAURA *and* MARK *put massive parcels on their heads and line up.* ROLAND *puts on a sun helmet and they embark on the Grand Safari of the Upper Cunt. They come across landmarks, evidence of previous doomed expeditions etc., etc. Improvise. Ultimately they recognise that the audience is a surrounding body of hostile tribesmen. They bombard them out of the theatre with tennis balls.*

ROLAND *(from the theatre door after their retreating backs).* And don't you come back, you Marxist, Maoist, Fascist, Taoist, Existentialist, shopping list pineapples. Sod off, you pink little squibs etc. etc. . .

People Show Number Christ
Knows How Many

People Show Number Christ Knows How Many was first performed at the Oval Theatre, October, 1972.

Performers: José Nava
Terry Day
Mark Long
Laura Gilbert

Music was provided on the opening night by Jeff Nuttall and Ian Hinchliffe

Space. *Audience in two blocks at right angles to each other, L-shaped.*

Centre–a domestic scene consisting of a table laid for tea and a toilet, with cistern if possible, which is also a drum-kit. A cymbal rises out of the bowl. Various bells etc. are hung around, and when it is pissed into the noise is amplified. The noise can be a tinkling or a drumming, as preferred. The milk jug on the table is large and contains blood.

In the corner opposite the audience a platform, suspended high, hung with pots and pans and the objects to be offered to LAURA, *which must be hung in such a way that they can be pulled down from below.* JOSÉ *can work on this and add anything else that he wants.*

Next to the platform a swing with ribbons. At the start the swing is attached to the platform so that LAURA *can use the platform as a jumping off point.*

Dress. LAURA *is a fierce bird. She has huge wings strapped on her shoulders, made of boxwood and flattened out tin. She has flaming make-up and body-paint and feathers on her head and anywhere else.*

MARK *wears morning dress, bowler hat, face completely covered in bandages. Wears gloves, and has his prick hanging out throughout the show.*

TERRY *is his wife, turban, mules, curlers, plastic pinny.* JOSÉ *is God alias Speedy Gonzalez. He wears a sexy ladies' nighty and long johns. Smokes a huge cigar perpetually.*

Audience enter. Everybody in position. MARK *and* TERRY *at table.* LAURA *and* JOSÉ *on platform. Housewife's Choice is coming from the radio. Audience settle.* TERRY *switches off radio.*

TERRY. I am not, definitely not, impressed. *(Switches radio on.)*
TERRY *(switches radio off).* I am not definitely not depressed *(Radio on.)*
TERRY *(radio off).* I am not, definitely not, undressed *(Radio on.)*
TERRY *(radio off).* I am not, definitely not, increased. *(Radio on)*
TERRY *(radio off).* I am not definitely not, released. *(Radio on)*
TERRY *(radio off).* I am not, definitely not, policed. *(Radio on)*

After each of these statements, just before the radio is turned on, MARK *makes a silly noise, with his voice, with a whistle, or with a tooter. Radio fades out.*

LAURA. Eagle squeaks! Hack your back on glass! *(Shrieks and swings down over table knocking over jug of blood.)*

Silence.

MARK. Messy bitch. What a way to come on!

Total dark. Mad bird sounds from the parrot house. Silence.
JOSÉ *illuminates his own face from below with a flash-lamp.*

JOSE. I am the fucking Father Almighty. That is who I am.

Table lamp goes on for MARK *and* TERRY.

MARK. I blame myself. It just seemed right at the time. And the grave didn't look like a grave. That's why I dug it circular, so it wouldn't look like a grave.
TERRY. And then the price went up.
JOSÉ. I am the fucking maker of Heaven and fucking Earth.
MARK. I'm totally responsible really. I never thought about is as a perversion. It never occurred to me that maybe there was something strange about a Daddy that wanted to see his little darling immersed in meringue.
TERRY. And then the manager came in.
JOSÉ. And Jesus Christ is my only son, by Christ!
MARK. I'm just greedy really. When I was small I used to go with my mother to the Khardoma and watch her eat meringue. All those comfy white botties disappearing into her little red hole. And then there was what my school chums and I used to call the meringue poultice but we won't go into that. *(Pause.)* After all, I've come into it perhaps too often.
TERRY. And then the war came.
MARK. If I'd been bolder and faster it wouldn't have been so bad. But it takes a good few hours to fill a grave with meringue and then when she wouldn't get in after that, well I felt so stupid . . .
TERRY. And that's just what Mr Churchill said.
MARK. I shouldn't have chased her like that. Uphill and down dale. Down Perseverance Street and up Temperance Row. Over the top and under the door. Down to the bottom and past the clock. Land and sea. Gas and air. Fire and brimstone. Marks and Spencer. Pinky and Perky. Morecambe and Wise. Fled away she did. Left her poor old dad stuck with a grave full of goo.
TERRY. And then your sister went into hospital.
JOSÉ. Born of the Virgin Sturgeon, suffered under Percy the Pirate, was crushed and fried, dead as a piece of pudding.
MARK. Wooden wings. Hearts of oak. Spirit of Trafalgar and Biggin Hill. Bat out of hell. All out for six. Ripping through the cumulus. What chance does a mortal meringue addict stand in the face of an airborn nymphet banging up to the stratosphere on a couple of kitchen doors? I ask you!
TERRY. God knows how we managed it. The Co-Op was a great help.

JOSÉ. He descended into Fucking Hell. The third day he got up out of bed. He came up here with me.

MARK. So I can call myself the inventor of a new phenomenon in space. When a Messerschmitt smashes down smack in your own backyard you'll know that you've suffered the accidental benefits resulting from my unfortunate obsessions.

TERRY. Still count your blessings, thank God.

JOSÉ. Think nothing of it–From whence we shall come to judge the butter and the bread. I am the Holy Cow, the Holy Carbolic Soap, the Community at large, the prostitution of the body and the life everlasting. So you better all fucking watch out, okay?

LAURA. Okay O-Q, O-P, O Piss, Oh fuckit! *(Dives again.* MARK *and* TERRY *on their faces under the table. Swing comes slowly to a stop.* LAURA *alights. Scratches her fanny, stretches, yawns . . .)* Oh well, time to say me prayers. *(Turns and shouts to* JOSÉ.*)* Our father!

JOSÉ. Yes! What do you want?

LAURA. Which art in Heaven. *(Still shouting.)*

JOSÉ. Well what d'you expect, a fucking penthouse?

LAURA. Hallowed by thy name.

JOSÉ. Hello to you too. Let's get past the formalities.

LAURA. Thy Kingdom come.

JOSÉ. My kingdom's already been and went. What else?

LAURA. Thy will be done.

JOSÉ. So you all better do as you're told. Okay, anything else?

LAURA. On earth as it is in Heaven.

JOSÉ. Baby, I can fix anything.

LAURA. Give us this day our daily bread.

JOSÉ. Money, money. All they ever want is money.

LAURA. And forgive us our trespasses as we forgive them that trespass against us.

JOSÉ. Okay, case dismissed.

LAURA. For thine is the kingdom, the power and the glory, forever and ever . . .

JOSÉ. You got it baby. You ain't seen nothin' yet. Now listen, I am going to tell you something. When it comes to glorious powers and powerful kingdoms all you motherfuckers got a lot to learn. And who is going to tell you? Who is it that has got the secret of how to run the universe on cut-price gasoline? Who is the man with a weapon. that sunk a thousand battleships? Who is the flash in the pan? The cuckoo in the nest? The proof of the pudding? The gilt on the gingerbread? The master arse bandit of the galaxies?

LAURA. Who was it then?

JOSÉ. It is I, Speedy Gonzalez.

Strobe. Thunderflashes. Gunfire. Screams. Whinnying horses. JOSÉ *fires six-guns from the platform.*

Lights up on wreckage. All that remains untouched is the platform and the drum-kit-toilet.

MARK *emerges, wanders furtively round. Guiltily takes out a condom and puts it on. He holds it on while he pisses into it. Calls* TERRY *out of the wreckage.* TERRY *emerges and starts to play the drum-kit.* MARK *takes off the condom, shakes his prick a bit, puts it away, zips it up. Takes a pin from his lapel and squeezes a series of bursts of piss onto the amplified drum, or whatever it is, in the toilet bowl.* LAURA *moves in abrupt mechanical movements all round the audience, a sort of clock-work dance. Event ends when condom is empty.*

MARK *(to* LAURA). Where the 'ell 'ave you been?

TERRY *continues punctuating this dialogue with drums.*

LAURA. Up in the sky.
MARK. Why did you depart?
LAURA. Up for a fly.
MARK. When will you come back to *(gestures towards* TERRY) me and your old lady?
LAURA. I'd have to be very needy.
MARK. Tell me, tell me, what–what did I do?
LAURA. You lost me to Speedy.
MARK. Speedy schmeedy. I've always been against religion.
LAURA. So I turned into a wood-pigeon.
MARK. It can't be true.
LAURA. Up your flue.

Drums cut out on rim shot.

LAURA *(to audience).* Now I want to tell you about my father. Are you sitting comfortably? Absolutely splendid.
My father, my father gets up to some very silly tricks.
When I was only five he shat in the bath and drowned my dolly.
When I was six he sat in a tree and showed his ingenuity.

MARK *tries on a series of outlandish hats.*

When I was seven he sat in the stove and sang football songs.

MARK *and* TERRY *sing* 'You'll Never Walk Alone'. *Audience join in.*

When I was eight he pulled all the light fittings out of the lawn and had worms installed in the hall.
When I was nine he adopted a West-Indian horse and fed it on all my old comics.
When I was ten he ran for the council.
When I was eleven he caight it and bought a balcony ticket to 'The Saga of Speedy Gonzalez'.
MARK. We had a ringside seat.
Speedy led with a mother and followed with a tit.

He rode a plastic engine through the second round and passed his eleven plus in a turd.
Three O-levels in Round Four and a packet of peanuts.
Two more in Round Five and a stick of candyfloss.
In Round Ten my daughter and I, immersed in meringue, witnessed the corruption of Speedy Gonzalez into a life of sexual excess.
I clapped, my daughter clapped, but when that which is perfect is come, those who suffer from the clap shall be blown away.
JOSÉ. Into the clouds, beyond the crows.
Sneezed by the Almighty Nose.
Seized by the throat and the underclothes.
Banged on the mountains and swallowed by six regiments of fascist flamingoes!
LAURA. That'll be enough of that. *(Mounts cycle.)* Have to be off again I fear. *(Rides round theatre ringing bell.)*
MARK, TERRY *(to the tune of* 'Daisy Belle')

Speedy Speedy
Give us an onion soon.
We're quite weedy
Not to say out of tune.
It won't be a turnip will it?
And we won't have to kill it.
And we'll get drunk
On spider spunk
And a slice of banana moon.

Speedy unrolls big pantomime song sheet with the words. Big sing song.

Suddenly JOSÉ *is in the audience–slightly before the end of the chorus–ten gallon hat, bandoliers, sérape etc. A chicken in his mouth. Hurls chicken into the audience.* MARK *and* TERRY *hide.* LAURA *continues cycling and ringing bell.* JOSÉ *tries to persuade her to come up to heaven. Offers her various attractions. A bucket of water. A rubber duck. A wellington. A telephone directory. A stuffed animal.* MARK *and* TERRY *emerge from the audience, one on either side. Encourage the audience to make sarcastic catcalls. Develops into a screaming row with* LAURA *and* JOSÉ *on one side and the audience on the other, which reaches a climax after which they both back out silently glaring.* MARK *and* TERRY *are on the platform.*

MARK *and* TERRY *(to the tune of* 'Daisy Belle').

Gracie Gracie
Give us your plaster pig.
We're so lazy
We can't stand things too big.
We're only two small potatoes.
We don't like fat policemen
But they look sweet
Upon the seat
Of a left-hand diesel-powered automatic fork-lift.

MARK *tells some signing off jokes and then, to the tune of* 'Just a Song At Twilight'.

MARK, TERRY Don't fall through the skylight
When you're on the roof.
Folks who fall through skylights
Never learn the truth
Don't believe the rumour
That the onion tells.
Only onions whisper
Like wedding bells
Like we–he–he–di–hing bells.

Lights dim out. Lights up for the Queen.

Oh the Birds, a People Show
(Trra!)

Oh the Birds, a People Show (Trra!) was performed at the Oval Theatre, Spring, 1973

Performers:	Laura Gilbert	Oozlum Bird
	Derek Wilson	Telegraph Pole
	Mark Long	Cold Chip
	José Nava	Eagle Puff
	Mike Figgis	Birdwatcher

Layout–chaotic–twigs and branches everywhere–bundles of hay and straw–no proper seats, only bits of old cars–effect of a dingle, a country rubbish dump–any mattresses should be wet–there should, in fact, be a good deal of wet, safer innit–trees, ladders and swings for the birds to play about in.

Mark is COLD CHIP *and looks the part–grey, rectangular, (cardboard?), cold fat.*

Laura is outrageous–lots of ostrich feathers and bright colours and no feet. She is the OOZLUM BIRD *that flies round in ever diminishing circles etc. etc. . . . Derek is static and hums. Other people's messages flow through him. Laura sits on his head much of the time. He is a* TELEGRAPH POLE. *José has swastikas and an eagle head and lovely make-up. He is* EAGLE PUFF. *Figgis is an enthusiastic* BIRDWATCHER. *Antiquated taperecorder and butterfly net.*

Scene 1.

OOZLUM BIRD. I am up my bum.
TEL. POLE. Absurd.
OOZLUM BIRD. They were chasing me–the Christmas Cracker,
 the Carpet Tack and Margaret Thatcher,
 Watching me for matches, flaming feathers,
 Washing leathers. Fooled the buggers. Slurp.
TEL. POLE. How bloody silly.
OOZLUM BIRD. From the depths of my bum I adore thee.
 I have always liked a good telephone pole.
 From the depths of my bowels I howl for thee.
 I have always fancied porcelain insulators.
 From the sink of the sphincter I fart thy name.
 I have always had a voice like a lovelorn euphonium.
 Come to me Telly Welly Holypole. I would not conceal
 myself from thee.
TEL. POLE. How revolting.
BIRDWATCHER. Hist!

Scene 2.

EAGLE PUFF *is poncing around all the time with Gay Lib banner and swastika on it. What a gentle eagle!*

BIRDWATCHER *(stalking him).* A rare one there. No feathers, more hair. If I draw close I'll scare him. Oh no, his name is not Jim, it is Eileen and he is a fierce queen, the fiercest queen I've ever seen.

OOZLUM BIRD. Here you old puff, d'you want to hide up my botty?

BIRDWATCHER. God knows where they disappear to. I looked at the Oozlum bird and away she flew. I'll never have an Oozlum for Bristol Zoo. The Wild West Show had one or two. Perhaps if I set a trap with glue.

OOZLUM BIRD. It's nice and cosy up here. It's the only place you can keep your feathers dry.

BIRDWATCHER. It is fabled in the land of Oozlum that a bird can hide up her own little bum. Or big bum for that matter. What's that? The smell of old fried batter?

COLD CHIP. Like a bit of life, bit of style. Very flash jungle this, very.

BIRDWATCHER. Great merciful heaven, it's a Cold Chip.

COLD CHIP. Like to feel nice and greasy, goes in easy.
I'm a maiden's pride and joy.
And they fly round back to front
With a cold chip up their. . .

BIRDWATCHER. I shall use the poor wrinkled little fucker as bait.

TEL. POLE. How pathetic.

Scene 3

BIRDWATCHER. Poor, poorpoor
Poor little cold chip, poor old chippy chappy.
I, oh yes I do, I and I alone,
Know how to make you huppy happy.
Jump in my net, poor underdeveloped little sod,
It's a bit of a chip pan and I'll play God
And carry you off without a word
To a land where a cold chip, so I've heard.
Might get his end up the Oozlum Bird.

COLD CHIP. Oo sounds well, sounds quite fair.
Hang on while I take a sec to grease my hair.
The Oozlum you say, now that can't be bad.
You know when it comes to birds I'm the lad.
I remember the day before I was fried
And there was a sparrer that tried and tried
To resist me, a spud new cut,
But she had to give in. I made her a slut,
I fear, but to hell with it, I don't care,
As long as I get 'em stripped down bare.
Not a bird in the jungle don't fancy a bit.
The bird that escapes me's a *very tough tit.*

OOZLUM BIRD. Two steaks in a Maidenform
And a pair of lips that were made for 'em.
TEL. POLE. Ouch!
BIRDWATCHER. I'm glad I've engaged your services, Chippy old chap.
Let's be off and we'll set our trap.

Scene 5.

BIRDWATCHER *and* COLD CHIP *attempt unsuccessfully to lure the* OOZLUM BIRD *off* TELEGRAPH POLE.

EAGLE PUFF. Ah-hah! *(Or words to the same effect.)*

Scene 6.

TEL. POLE. I am not prepared to take part in any of this rubbish.
BIRDWATCHER. Oh I see, well what about the green helicopter?
TEL. POLE. Green helicopter is a silly thing to say.
BIRDWATCHER. Well, er–what about snotty cabbage?
TEL. POLE. I really don't see the point of this sort of thing.
BIRDWATCHER. How about fried fly?
TEL. POLE. It's really no good you blathering on.
BIRDWATCHER. Do you deny the tractor sink?
TEL. POLE. What does this show do for Women's Lib?
BIRDWATCHER. Or the railway table?
TEL. POLE. Or Student Grants?
BIRDWATCHER. Or the Camberwell camels?
TEL. POLE. Or the Legalise Pot Campaign?
BIRDWATCHER. Or even the Oozlum Bum?
TEL. POLE. Or community work?
BIRDWATCHER. Or the sniggering bucket?
TEL POLE. Or the Black Panthers?
BIRDWATCHER. Or the National Birdwatchers' Association?
TEL. POLE. Or the Rent Act?
BIRDWATCHER. Or Civil Defence?
TEL. POLE. Or the Industrial Relations Court?
BIRDWATCHER. Or Piddly Poo's Plop Plops, eh?
OOZLUM BIRD. I've got a grip on a lovely cold chip.
COLD CHIP. Oh very fair, very fair indeed.

Scene 8.

COLD CHIP. I would like to interrupt this load of completely irresponsible infantile self-indulgence by Jeff Nuttall to ask you, each one of you, what spirit you bring to a public place when you visit it. Do you still walk the streets armed with an indignation that will refuel our flagging energies? Do you lie beside your lover with a caring love that will enoble the clichés of the dirty bookshops and the avant-garde stage? Do you still touch one anothers' fingers with a sense that the touching of fingers is a quicksilver flowing exclusively through human veins? When you kiss does the quality of light still invade your human bodies, or do your lips and loins merely grope in the dark and the stench of the casual pad for more sensation to see you through to the next deal? Do you still buy fruit to charm your love? Do you still walk with her through oilier walks of Regent's Park? Have you a spark to light the flight of taxicabs, the all-pervading flock of cars that carry us to soapy bars? Have you forgotten the promises you made to Gopy Mopes and Gleepy Meeps and Gluppity Pob? Oh do not, do not become a mob of petrol pumps or discarded shoes. Even now we cannot lose. The Enchanted Laundromat is ashattered for us all and we, we can eat the luminous machinery.

Scene 8.

OOZLUM BIRD. I've got a pong and a drip
And an old pink slip
And a lot of old rubber
And a handful of blubber
And a sea of soap
And a deal of dope
And the Band of Hope
And a sexy grope
And a big ripe plum
In my cosy bum.
BIRDWATCHER, TEL. POLE. Remarkable, remarkable.
COLD CHIP. I've tried it endways on
With a man called Ron
And diagonal farts
With Lionel Bart
And frontal attack
In a canvas sack
And abdominal sag
In a sleeping bag
But I've never enjoyed such a comfy drum
As Oozlum's psychedelic bum.
BIRDWATCHER, TEL. POLE. And they look so lovely together.
OOZLUM BIRD. I've got a kitchen sump
And a hydraulic pump
And a pair of dice

And sugar mice
And an attack of lice
And a reasonable price
And an automatic flush
And Basil Brush
And a difficult sum
In my Oozlum Bum.

BIRDWATCHER, COLD CHIP. A splendid collection. Oh yes.

COLD CHIP. I've been bubbled in fat
I've been where it's at
I've been chewed with beans
In some sordid scenes
I've been served with eggs
And chickens' legs
I've snuggled close
To soggy toast
But even a rissole in golden crumbs
Was never as tasty as Oozlum's Bum.

BIRDWATCHER, TEL. POLE. A remarkable specialist knowledge.

EAGLE PUFF. Aahah. *(Or some similar expression.)*

Scene 9.

EAGLE PUFF *chops down* TEL. POLE, *tortures* BIRDWATCHER, *eats* COLD CHIP.

Scene 10.

The Wedding of EAGLE PUFF *and* OOZLUM BIRD. *Organ music, the lot.*

Harriet Piecebeam and the Mice

Harriet Piecebeam and the Mice was performed at the Oval Theatre, later at the Cockpit Theatre, London, and thence on tour, during 1973-4.

Performers included	Stephen Rea
Caroline Hutchison
Cecily Hobbs
Neil Goodrun

Stephen Rea directed

Space. *Chairs are placed so that they project in rows out from the walls of the theatre. The rows should be at least five feet away from one another. The seats should be all facing forward, front to back, front to back, like in a bus. The effect should be that some silly person has been playing with them.*

Characters. WINNIFRED WHITETHORN–*she wears a dress reminiscent of past splendours–maybe as though for Henley or Ascot. A bunch of celery is tied to her cheek with a pink ribbon. The hat should be designed to accommodate for this if she wears one.*

SLASHER–*He wears an amalgamation of Rocker gear. He has a live mouse sellotaped to the back of each hand, and maybe others elsewhere.*

FRIENDLY GEORGE–*he wears pyjamas torn at the crutch so that his prick occasionally shows. He carries a half demolished teddy bear.*

SUSAN *and* EDNA–*are bandaged firmly back to back. They wear cheap Mickey Mouse masks and* EDNA *has a light wooden chair tied firmly to her left leg.*

1. SUSAN *and* EDNA *are rolling around the floor as the audience comes in. When everybody is in a brass band starts to play and all action stops until the brass band stops.*

2. WINNIFRED *is singled out with a spot. She says:* 'My name is Winnifred Whitethorn. I think my name is Winnifred Whitethorn I feel at liberty to say my name is Winnifred Whitethorn.' *Then the brass band plays again and everything is stock still.*

3. GEORGE, *who has been outside so far, bangs on the door. He says:* 'Is that Harriet Piecebeam?'
WINNIFRED *says:* 'Yes it is.' *The brass band plays again and all stand stock-still.*

4. GEORGE *knocks again. He says:* 'Well where d'you want me to leave this torpedo?' WINNIFRED *says:* 'My name is Winnifred Whitethorn.' *The brass band plays again and all action stops.*

5. WINNIFRED *says:* 'My name is not Winnifred Whitethorn. My name is Harriet Piecebeam.' *The name* Harriet Piecebeam *winks on in fairy bulbs. She goes on:* 'And I love to be alive and so terribly terribly talented.' *The brass band again and no action.*

6. *A bucket of water tips over* WINNIFRED. *She cries loudly like a spoiled child and walks out of the spotlight. Wherever she walks*

SUSAN *and* EDNA *follow her, wriggling along the floor like a clumsy fish.* SLASHER, *spotlit, follows them with a fishing net.* SLASHER *says* 'Nah then, nah then. Stop all dat splashin' abaht. On yer feet then. You'll ruin yer new tights.'
SUSAN *and* EDNA *say, in unison:* 'We flood the sleepy shallows of your liquid aspirations.'
SLASHER. 'You'll do nothing of the kind, you silly little cows. Come out of that thin Windsor soup.'
SUSAN, EDNA. 'We slither our silvan forms along the shadow of your dream streams.'
SLASHER. 'Don't be so bleedin' wet. 'ow do I know anythin' ahabt wet dreams? '
SUSAN, EDNA. 'Sing with us.'
SLASHER. 'I'll fump yer ear'oles.'
SUSAN, EDNA. 'Swim with us, swim with us, immortal amphibean.'

A bucket of water tips over SLASHER. *Brass band and all action stops.*

7. *Spotlight on* WINNIFRED. *She says:* 'It's not really funny. I used to look at him afterwards. "George, friendly George, you're crying," I would say. One night I threw the window open onto the street so that everyone would know. "He's crying," I screamed. He didn't hit me. I dreamed about him last night.'
GEORGE. 'What did you dream about me?'
WINNIFRED. 'I dreamed your eyes were little animals and they didn't belong to you.'
GEORGE. 'What I am supposed to do at that? Bust into tears again?'
WINNIFRED. 'And the animals could see things but they wouldn't tell you what they saw.'
GEORGE. 'Fish were they, these animals of yours?'
WINNIFRED. 'Not mine Friendly George, yours. And not fish, Friendly George, mice.'
GEORGE. 'For God's sake don't be so boringly melodramatic.'

The brass band plays while SLASHER, SUSAN *and* EDNA *walk through the audience slapping fish everywhere.* WINNIFRED *shouts:* 'Wrong, wrong. Mice. No, not fish, mice. You've got it wrong.'

8. SLASHER. 'We don't mess abaht wiv girls, us lot. No time for girls dahn the garage.'
SUSAN. 'And the grains of sugar falling on my naked body felt like the fingernails of starbeams.'
EDNA. 'They waited in the cattle trucks with no food or sanitatation for two days.'
GEORGE. 'All I wanted from you was a cup of cocoa and a blow job.'
SLASHER. 'Axel grease, that's what I'd give 'em. Fuckin' axel grease.'

WINNIFRED. 'No, mice, mice, I'm afraid.'
EDNA. 'And the sun sinks at great speed like a drowning drunk.'
WINNIFRED. 'Mice I tell you.'
SUSAN. 'Treacle sinks slowly into every crevice, slowly and warmly like a setting sun.'
GEORGE. 'I would have been happy with a mouthful of knickers out of the laundry basket.'
WINNIFRED. 'For God's sake, don't you know a mouse when you see one?'
SUSAN. 'And the mice come out to nibble my sticky labia. Kettle tops.'
EDNA. 'The whole train was infested with vermin. A sleeping child was blinded by mice.'
SLASHER. 'Mouse traps up 'em, the 'ole bleedin' lot.'
WINNIFRED. 'Mice you see. Very fine incisors.'
SLASHER. ' 'Eadache. Suddink crawlin' abaht in me petrol tank.'
SUSAN. 'My pores are watching me feed. How they love one another!'
WINNIFRED. 'Mouseholes!'
EDNA. 'Escape tunnels!'
SLASHER. 'Exhaust pipes!'
GEORGE. 'Arseholes!'
SUSAN. 'Fuck me, fuck me!'

And then there is an explosion.

9. WINNIFRED *and* GEORGE *are fucking on the floor. There is a dim light and organ music. Their movements follow the spasmodic rhythms of their speech.*

WINNIFRED. 'You're humiliating me, you know that.'
GEORGE. 'I'm sorry. I can't help it. Some things have to come to pass.'
WINNIFRED. 'Every driving thrust drives me back into my cradle.'
GEORGE. 'My darling, you know I'd follow you even there.'
WINNIFRED. 'I wish I hadn't been born.'
GEORGE. 'I wish I could make you want to live.'
WINNIFRED. 'Oh you silly bastard. You with your messianic Willie.'
GEORGE. 'I'm just an ordinary bloke.'
WINNIFRED. 'You're just like them all.'
GEORGE. 'My name is Friendly George.'

SLASHER *slams door five times.*

WINNIFRED. 'My name is Winnifred Whitethorn. My name is Winnifred Whitethorn. My name is Winnifred Whitethorn.
SUSAN, EDNA. 'And the government planted daffodils over the collective grave.'

WINNIFRED. 'How much longer are you going to go on? It's worse than Sunday afternoon.'
GEORGE. 'But–but I come alive again on Sunday afternoon.'
WINNIFRED. 'Why must you always destroy me?'
GEORGE. 'I need spiritual food.'
WINNIFRED. 'You are a lecherous impotent ass.'
GEORGE. 'Once, in Cairo, there was–a–a–sideshow. I paid four francs to see. . .
WINNIFRED. 'Have you completed the radio payments?'
SUSAN, EDNA. 'Oy, where d'ya want this torpedo?'

A brass band plays and all stand to attention.

10.*The entire cast are in a row,* SLASHER *central. Effect of music hall lighting, green to blue for* SLASHER's *speeches, bright for the chorus. At every chorus the* 'Harriet Piecebeam' *sign winks behind them.*

SLASHER. 'At the sinking of the fat mouse and the rising of the earthworm we will remember them. At the singing of the anthem and the sharp cry of the tulip we will remember them. O antediluvian ape, grace us with thy pendulant saliva.'
COMPANY *(to the tune of* 'Get Out and Get Under').
'Ya gotta grab amber
Ya gotta grab amber
Ya gotta chew celery peel.'
SLASHER. 'And I never hear her now unless through slamming doors that resonate a pearl of avocado in a trice. And still I turn to yester tree and scare the birds that climb the terraces of chairs and leap about and die.'
COMPANY. 'Ya go to the seaside,
Go boppin' on bromide
And wind down the window for tea.'
SLASHER. 'And the night falls and the tree falls and the bird falls and the curtain falls and the bad man falls and the Indian falls and morality falls and the temperature falls and Niagra Falls and Victoria Falls and Albert Hall and Edward Road and Alexandra Terrace and Mafeking Avenue and make a king 'ave a sweet and avabanana and avocado avocado. Evening drops down blue as a virgin's tooth.'
COMPANY. 'Goodnight everybody.
Goodnight everybody.
Goodnight everybody, goodnight.'
WINNIFRED. My name is Winnifred Whitethorn.'

A brass band plays. When it has finished, they all bow and walk off.

Producer's note: The main thing about this piece is its formality. Because it makes no sense, the sheer form of it is deeply important. Therefore improvisations and additions should not detract from its formality. All written words should be word perfect. Sound and audibility are very important.

The Visit

The Visit was performed at the Oval Theatre,
The Howff, London, and thence on tour during
1973-4.

Performers: Stephen Rea
Caroline Hutchison
John Mitchell
Cecily Hobbs
Kevin Heath
Caroline Satchell

Stephen Rea directed

Act One.

Audience is seated in rows in front of the loudspeakers. The action takes place in the aisles. Chairs and buckets are used for different levels.

The armchair, wherever it is, should be raised. Complete dark.

LOUDSPEAKER. It is a major philosophical problem attached to the whole therapeutic field to decide whether or not a human being is a history of behaviour or a limitless truth presenting a series of lies about itself.

GEORGE *stands up in the audience naked in a spotlight hitting himself over the head with a big floppy rubber object of his own choosing. Complete dark.*

LOUDSPEAKER. If the first is untrue then the behaviour of a murderer who, in his murderous action, is merely pretending a murderous desire, is unimportant, whilst, if the second is untrue, one may look for no hidden motive, and murder in no way registers a dislike of the victim.

ALICE *in party frock and Alice-band lies drunk in the armchair. Slowly, finding it awkward because of the beer bottle she holds and spills, she pulls up her dress and pulls down her knickers. The spotlight which illuminates her narrows down until she is completely in shadow except for her hairless cunt. As the light narrows a long sound somewhere between a sigh and a sung note follows the narrowing of the beam. Lights up when she says:*

ALICE *(to* LIONEL*).* Eat me.

LIONEL *feverishley opens a bag of crisps and eats them. Complete dark.*

LOUDSPEAKER. If the first is true a satisfactory cure for a thief would be to tie his hands firmly to his sides. If all potential and proven thieves spent their lives either so handicapped or amputated the level of loss in supermarkets and public gardens would be considerably reduced.

If the second contention is true then all we need do with people professing not to be thieves is to call their bluff by cutting off their hands.

Lights up for a game of blind man's buff for the entire cast while a Strauss waltz plays very loudly. Complete dark.

LOUDSPEAKER. In any case why should I pretent to you to be a voice in the dark. It would surely be more honest if I were to offer myself (*a*) as a series of interlocked spheres.

Flash of MAUREEN, *bucket on head, festooned with old metal spoons, skipping. The dark.*

LOUDSPEAKER. (*b*) as a woollen rabbit miraculously enlivened by the passing gales of Godly heartburn.

Flash of GEORGE *masturbating. Dark.*

LOUDSPEAKER. I know the difficulties some of you encountered in coming here this evening. I know the terrible speed with which the wheels of buses and taxi-cabs crush the appealing faces of the little snails who seek nothing but their birthday presents in the rainy early evening light. I know the commissionaires with stones in their eyes and the Trafalgar lion with contact lenses. Because I know these things I would ask you to examine the current psychiatric situation with more than ordinary diligence. Take for instance this situation.

Fade in Housewives' Choice music while the lights go up on the following scene. LIONEL *sellotapes crisps to* ALICE's *face and left leg until they are completely covered. She intersperses a muttered improvised monologue with snatches from* 'The Maid of the Mountain' *while he does it. The monologue concerns the day she ate the kittens. This action continues while* GEORGE *and* ROXANNE *carry out the following dialogue.*

GEORGE *(with newspaper).* Alright then, what time's 'er train?
ROXANNE *(slicing carrots).* What d'you care what time 'er train is?
GEORGE. Well you want me to go down and collect the old boot din't you?
ROXANNE. My mother, my *mother,* is more than an old boot.
GEORGE. A bloody wellington—with spurs.
ROXANNE. My mother is a dignified professional woman.
GEORGE. Dignified? Dignified? So's the Queen 'avin' a shit.
ROXANNE. Oh you're vulgar, you are.
GEORGE. I believe in speaking my mind.
ROXANNE. No wonder yer breath smells.
GEORGE. 'ow long is she stayin' anyway?
ROXANNE. What's it to you?
GEORGE. What's it to me? You try kippin' in that bleedin' armchair.
ROXANNE. My mother and I need some time alone together. We was always very close.
GEORGE. Close? Close? I think you got your foot caught.
ROXANNE. Foot caught? What d'you mean? Where?

GEORGE. Up 'er–You know–Up 'er wotsit.
ROXANNE *(says nothing).*
GEORGE. I reckon you never made it. I reckon you're a deprived person sadly lacking the foot you left be'ind up the old maternal orifice.
ROXANNE. You've got a peculiar idea of women, you 'ave.
GEORGE. Your mother is a peculiar woman. She walks peculiar. . . as though she 'ad a foot stuck up 'er. . .
ROXANNE. She can't 'elp 'ow she walks.
GEORGE. Bleedin' right she can't. You'd walk funny with some bugger's foot up yer.
ROXANNE. Ah well, a foot'd be somethin' these days.
GEORGE. Oh we're on that now, are we? Five minutes before the Nazi invasion and you go all nympho on me.
ROXANNE. Nympho? Blimey. Good job I ain't. That'd be a waste of bleedin' time that would, wouldn't it?
GEORGE. Well you can cuddle up with yer mum. I always thought there was somethin' bent goin' on there.
ROXANNE. Bent? Bent? There's only one thing that won't come out straight in this 'ouse.
GEORGE. Well, tell you the truth, there's a reason you know.
ROXANNE. Too right there's reason. Premature senility.
GEORGE. Long words eh?
ROXANNE. There's nothing wrong with length.
GEORGE. That's why your mother stays such a bleedin' long time.
ROXANNE. My mother can stay as long as she likes.
GEORGE. Your mother can drop dead.
ROXANNE. Are you goin' to fetch 'er then?
GEORGE. I asked yer–what time's the bleedin' train?
ROXANNE. It gets there in about fifteen minutes time.

Train whistle. Lights out–a snatch of 'Chattanooga Choo Choo'

LOUDSPEAKER. The situation can be assessed either in terms of time or in terms of emotion. If the problem is one of time it divides rather neatly into two.
(a) How can George and Roxanne extend their domestic repartee even further so as to take up every spare moment of the day and night fully and
(b) whether or not George can get to the station in time is a question that can largely be left in the hands of the local police. If, on the other hand, the problem is emotional it can only be solved by love. It is to this end that the ensuing ritual is devoted.

Lights up.

GEORGE *(imitating a motor car as he moves round the room).* Brumm. Brumm. Toot toot. Brmmmmmm. I like a gear lever you can get your 'and round. *(Hits* MAUREEN's *bucket in passing.)*

ALICE. Daddy's Lagonda's got a lollypop love. *(Hits bucket.)*
MAUREEN. For fuck's sake leave me alone.
LIONEL. Or perhaps in a song and a single undergarment. Why not a dog? *(Hits bucket.)*
ALICE. And Spot's got a lollypop. Moves into third ever tho thmoothly.
ROXANNE. I hope he drives gently. She can't stand vibrations.
GEORGE. Brmm brmm. Peep peep. There's the old station where we used to click.
LIONEL. Or military knickers. The day on the downs. Got out of the car, hockey shorts and bare tits. Ran, old chap, *ran* into the sun.
GEORGE. One or another– WAAFS, ATS. Military briefs dragging in the blackout. Khaki directoire, flannel or rayon. Peep peep brmm. Bloody-well brummmm.
ROXANNE. Remember the day he ran over a cat.
ALICE. I sit on a mirror. Look at the run-over pussy-cat, split.
ROXANNE. Sticky and dark out there. They're late.
ALICE. On my back with my legs in the air, flashing the gash in the pussy-cat's tummy.
GEORGE. Stretched on the sleepers, Brmmm, back of the Goods Yard Brmmm. Last train back to camp. Sunday night. Peeep.
LIONEL. If I dare take a peek when she's swathed in metal–
ALICE. I clatter about like a rat in a trap–
GEORGE. Roxanne and the dragon–They'll yatter away till the small hours–
ALICE. Faster and faster. The dead cat gasps.
ROXANNE. He can never grasp that she is my mother–
LIONEL. –Or rust and rasping in dirty tin. . .
GEORGE. If she's been waiting she's going to be mad–
ALICE. My cat's mad and there's too much blood–
LIONEL. Red is the colour of her best Maserati–
GEORGE. Red is the colour of her eye in anger–

Train whistle. All stop and pause.

ALICE. Just playing mummy. What's for tea?

Lights out. Audience go out for first interval.

Act Two

Seats are regrouped in sets of three or four, irregularly positioned as though at a party or informal meeting. GEORGE *comes on wearing a false nose.*

GEORGE. Ladies and bog hoppers. Bag snatchers and snatch grabbers, gentlemen and fly-fingerers, napkin straddlers and laundromat gobble queens, I come before you tonight not as a performing reptile with afflicted skin, nor yet as an unexplored planet with galactic leanings. My task is simple, so simple Simon wouldn't tell the Pieman, and the Pieman wouldn't have told the Peaman if he'd known, and the Peaman wouldn't have told the Cabbage Man or the Lettuce Lover. Which leads me to say that if no one amongst you tonight is a lettuce lover, there's no need to panic. Tormented gentlemen wishing to wrap the member for Worthing in a limp lettuce leaf turn their attention to the tattered tulle, the fragrant fragments of mauled muslin surrounding the delectable diaphragm of that atomic little lady of song—Flash Alice!

ALICE *comes on. Her party dress is torn off one shoulder and she looks subtly tarty, maybe a touch of eye make-up.* MAUREEN *leaps around the space beating her bucket. The song* ALICE *sings should be wistful, romantic, and aimlessly improvised.*

ALICE *(singing).* I don't know why I should want to talk to people like you anyway.
I couldn't expect you to know the odours that come from a musty carpet where somebody called you once lay.
I couldn't expect you to know the address
Or why some girls' love lives get in a mess.
Or what to do when the door slams and you're left looking at the light fitting
And your nerves are like mad butterflies fluttering and flittering.
I don't want to tell you particularly
About the sensation when a relative with bad breath licks your early
Breasts and blows through your first fine hair as though he were cooling tea.
I don't believe any of you have any real interest in a case of grubby innocence like me.
So you might as well go sailing in your own boat across your own sea,
But when you get to the isle of your dreams
Don't be surprised if the heavenly music is punctuated with nasty screams
And when the god with the kind smile brings the magic cup for you to drink
Don't be surprised if he takes off his mask with a lear and a wink
And as you take the magic cup
You recognise that it's only Uncle George come to touch you up.

MAUREEN *beats her bucket twice after every rhyme in the song.*

GEORGE. Thank you Flash Alice. *(ALICE goes off.)* I don't have to tell you, lords and baubles, ladies and brine bibbers, what happened to poor dear Alice after the interference. There was so much, *so much* clutter on her radio channels that they had to dredge her on 205 meters and she finished up as a dry dock for soft submarines. Massive catches of Levantine lizards writhed around her urethra pursuing the whisps of maidenhood, hollowed out, dried out, melted down, blown away in a confusion of labyrinthine testicles. Let us consult the voice of Uncle George's guardian gorgon.

Pool of light on GEORGE *and* ROXANNE. *A kitchen table replaces the armchair. They pour tea endlessly and spectacularly from varying heights, with two or three teapots and a great many cups and saucers. The tea should be hot so that it steams. They do this while the* LOUDSPEAKER *speaks.*

LOUDSPEAKER *(*ROXANNE's *mother's voice).* Oh it wasn't easy, oh no. My stomach's never been the same since the change. *(Pause for laugh.)* The slightest thing, a road accident, a rape, a day trip to Hanoi, anything can send it spinning. The doctor calls it a gastric emergency and I wouldn't touch my tongue to what I call it. I wouldn't touch my tongue to half the food they bring up nowadays. Up goes the hatch, out of the darkness everything pours, with chips, peas, chopped carrots, nasty rumours, downright lies, unpleasant effluvia. Nothing can sooth your troubled parts. My liver, *my liver,* is a catherine wheel of agony in its own orbit. I used to be fit but I can't stand the look of the milkman's horse nor the sound of a diesel shaft.

ROXANNE. With a *child.*

GEORGE. Look, I only. . .

ROXANNE. Do you know the state of a girl's nerves at that age?

GEORGE. Sharp as a sparrow's nose.

ROXANNE. Oh how *could* you?

MAUREEN *(popping up at the back).* With his wobbly winky, the silly old sod.

LOUDSPEAKER *(*ROXANNE's *mother).* And when I saw the wreck of a man she hung around her neck at the time when the youth was fresh as little new cherry buns on her peaky-cheeks, when I saw him waiting by the ticket barrier, trying to pretend he was glad I'd come, I wondered why I'd suffered the journey. The circus performance I had from my breast to my buttocks, the suffering I'd undergone from Much Griping to Small Piping, was rewarded as usual by a set of false teeth in a face like an old sanitary towel. Oh I could die when he kisses me. My cheek was wet as a baby's lip for whole minutes with the touch of his teeth. I could hardly struggle to the car, I was so knocked over by the bad habits on his breath. Oh she made a mistake did our Roxanne. She's made an error there's no adjusting. And she was so pretty in her birthday frock. . .

ROXANNE. And tore her pretty dress.

GEORGE. It was an accident.
ROXANNE. And chewed her pink ribbon.
GEORGE. I was fond of the child.
ROXANNE. And gave her a shilling to–
GEORGE. To what?
ROXANNE. To lick your fingers afterwards.
GEORGE. Well there was no soap.
MAUREEN *(popping up).* Salty paws, salty paws.
Jesus Christ, the state of 'im.
LOUDSPEAKER (ROXANNE's *mother).* We were very close,
Roxanne and I.
He stands between us scratching his fly.
He's a limp intruder silent and grey.
She's never got in the family way
So he's not much good, that's plain to see.
He's the final twig on his family tree.
He's the very last gasp of anything at all
And to think, it was for him she had to fall.
It's a bloody long drop if you ask me
From her mother's lap to the likes of he.
She's far from happy, I can tell from her eyes,
And from the looks of him he's barely alive.
I can't help feeling there's something unsaid.
She's tense as wire when we're lying in bed
And I'm going to ask her what can be wrong.
It must be something that George brought along.
ROXANNE. She was crying for hours you know.
GEORGE. Well, it's her age.
ROXANNE. I wonder what you'll have to say when your victims get younger.
GEORGE. I've always been fond of tots.
ROXANNE. Animal!
MAUREEN *(popping up).* All fuckin' pigs if you ask me. *(Beats her bucket.)*
LOUDSPEAKER (ROXANNE's *mother).* So I was glad to get out of the house, glad to shake the dust. No joy to me to ring their doorbell. Five hours travelling for nothing. Every time I go I get more upset. It wouldn't be so bad if he'd ever speak. He's ruined her life; she'll come to nothing now. When he saw me to the train he didn't even wave. I shan't go again, unless of course I'm sent for.
ROXANNE. And what about the way you treated my mother?
GEORGE. Oh piss off.
ROXANNE. I've a damn good mind to go for good.
GEORGE. That's right, piss off.

MAUREEN *kicks her bucket across the room.*

GEORGE *(moving amongst the audience).* It amounts to a question of which is worth most. A balanced and happy productive life or a moment when you sell the whole lot for a peep at what's on the other side of the sunset. I've never been a poetic bloke. I've never wasted much time on sunsets and grand passions. It's Roxanne really who gave me the chance. I'm not the sort to chase anything that doesn't naturally fall my way in the natural order of things, if you see what I mean. . .(ALICE *is moving amongst the audience also, singing to herself.)* It was Roxanne and her mother who starved me so badly I was driven out of the dull routine of things—just for a minute. And I should be sorry, I suppose. She was upset—afterwards. But she knows, you see. She knows what I know and after she's finished her snivelling and tale-telling, when she's finally got back to her old position in the world and shown her mummy and daddy and Lionel and Joan and all the other ordinary uncles that she can still be the same little girl, she'll smell her flesh on a summer night and she'll lie in a trance breathing the dust from an old carpet, and that's not a bad present from kind Uncle George for pretty little Alice to turn in her mind as her life gets dim and uniform.

MAUREEN *(popping up).* Dirty old bastard.

Everybody goes out, MAUREEN *last, noisily.*

Act Three

Chairs are isolated and evenly spaced. All chairs are facing different ways.

Dark. Entire cast is distributed around the space, each with a differently pitched whistle and a powerful hand-torch; all naked.

LOUDSPEAKER (LIONEL's *voice).* Oh I forgive the child. Meek and mild chasing butterflies. Fluttering petticoats. I am going to paint a little watercolour using Uncle George for a brush. I shall probably entertain the simpering disasters to tea. Greed is mine. Turpentine. Sugar and meringue. Budgerigar's fangs. Toffee canaries. Not to worry.

ROXANNE *lights up her nose and mouth.* LIONEL *blows his whistle.*

LOUDSPEAKER (MAUREEN's *voice).* Christ Almighty. Bleedin' toenails Seen the lot now. Tell yer what, listen 'ere mate. Fair do's, bein' quite frank, seein' it's you, not that I'd say this every day, very occasionally, speakin' as one who knows, from the 'orse's mouth, pig's arse, elephant's ear, lion's share, hedgehog's snorkle, between you and me, go and get fucked.

GEORGE *lights his ear.* ROXANNE's *whistle.*

LOUDSPEAKER
(ALICE's *voice).* Dance with me Lionel. I shall do a recitation.
(LIONEL's *voice).* I love the movement of the tiny folds at your armpit.
(ALICE's *voice).* Here it is. Marigold marigold. Cheesemould cheesemould. Half a pepper young and old. Go to the shop immediately.
(LIONEL's *voice).* I shall not listen to another measure. What wind!
(ALICE's *voice).* Go to the high downs, dance on the low downs, derry downs.
(LIONEL's *voice).* I am learning how to decorate a mountain.

LIONEL *lights his knee.* ALICE's *whistle.*

LOUDSPEAKER (GEORGE's *voice).* Well I mean to say, I don't mean to be mean, but what I mean is that I didn't mean nothing, didn't mean no harm. It's mean of the world to think I'm mean, I mean to say, I didn't mean to scare the kid. I would have been mean to ignore the kid. And she was very free with it you know. Nothing mean about her.

ROXANNE *lights her left nipple.* LIONEL *blows his whistle.*

LOUDSPEAKER
(LIONEL's *voice).* Yes, but what does all that really mean?
(GEORGE's *voice).* It's alright for you. You've still got your looks and your catapult. Never slept with a dead walrus. Never had it off with a post bag. Penitential, I'll tell yer.
(LIONEL's *voice).* Yes, but what is it all for?
(GEORGE's *voice).* Finger in the Christmas cake. Bit of pink icing under yer nail. Go to sleep. Stick your nose in a little fat violet.
(LIONEL's *voice).* Yes, but how does one start?

ALICE *lights up her shaven cunt.* GEORGE's *whistle.*

LOUDSPEAKER (MAUREEN's *voice).* Never breathe a word. Rely on me. Your only friend. Whenever you need one. Whenever you don't need one, that's what I say. Quiet as a mouse. Won't say a dicky bird, know what I mean?

LIONEL *lights his buttocks.* ALICE's *whistle.*

LOUDSPEAKER (ROXANNE's *voice).* I am the only person here with any sense. I'm the only sensible thing about this whole situation. Now I want you all to take a long cool look at yourselves. Has it ever been worth it? All these insects in your underclothes, all these destructive sensations? I shall serve tea in half an hour and I shall expect you all to be there, neatly dressed and properly behaved. Now if someone will just apply a feather duster to my. . . *(fade out.)*

ROXANNE *lights up her pubic hair.* ALICE's *whistle.*

LOUDSPEAKER *(*ALICE's *voice, singing as before).* I collect small coloured objects and I put them in water.

Lights up slowly as characters move into the winding dance. Yards of material have been spread around the place, over and around the audience. Characters wind themselves in it by slow circling motions throughout ALICE's *song. At the end of the song everyone is fully draped.*

LOUDSPEAKER (ALICE's *voice).* I admire the colours. I'm a quite attentive daughter.
In liquid the music comes out in gleams
And jewels stand out on my stocking seams
And my tongue remembers sugary creams
That run down the stairs in long slow streams.
I shall go out in the morning air
And wash my lungs with the dew in my hair.
I shall soil my clothing, I don't care.
I shall never never go home for tea.
I shall never never dance on Uncle George's knee.
I shall dance on his belly and lie on his leg
And drink his harvest down to the dregs.
I'll drink his wine and dance his song
For nothing in the whole wide world lasts long.
Uncle George is sitting on a cloud
With the sun up his bum and he shouts out loud
Who's coming down to the woods for a walk
Or down on the carpet for a daisy stalk?
I'll be late for tea and my knife and fork
Will be laid out ready for a plate of pork.
I'll eat Uncle Pig and his fruity sauce
That's the same as the ice cream on the stairs of course,
And we'll mount the stairs to the golden attic
And I'm afraid our joy will be automatic.
So goodbye, goodbye wonderful dream.
I'm afraid I'm just what I've always seemed,
A terrible girl with a terrible eye
And a terrible Uncle George. Goodbye.

Jack Show–The Pig Show

Jack Show–The Pig Show was performed at the Studio of the University Theatre, Newcastle as part of the Newcastle Festival, 1972.

Performers: Jeff Nuttall
Rose McGuire

Co-written with Rose McGuire

There is a dummy with a pig's head (real one). JEFF's *cornet hangs from the ceiling.* ROSE *cuts open sections of the dummy and takes out various objects. The action is determined/suggested by the objects.* JEFF *plays audience in on cornet.*

Section One

Food–rotten vegetables, scrambled egg, tinned mincemeat etc. There is a raised platform–table and two chairs. Table is set. Platform possibly decorated.

ROSE *takes out food which is in polythene bags with little holes in them and throws them to the table. Once food is in the area* JEFF *'serves' it.* ROSE *joins him.*

JEFF. Ah Rose, a fragrance this evening, a rare fragrance. Is that (no, surely?) an egg that spangles your most inestimably fragile earlobe?
ROSE. You have a pert turn of phrase Sir John, if nothing superior to a turned fruit.
JEFF. Pommes de mousettes vertes peut-etre?
ROSE. Oh Sir John, oh dear dear Sir Roland. . . Get fucked.
JEFF. I can't stand these long mauve evenings.
ROSE. I sustain them in my long mauve negligee.

Improvise

JEFF. A negligible urge besets my entrails.
ROSE. Ah, il fait que c'est seulement l'indigestion. Oeuf? *(Throws egg in* JEFF's *face.)*
JEFF. I never see the sun sink behind the papier maché cedars without the strongest pang of remorse.

Improvise

ROSE. Poor Edna. Poor poor poor dear dear Edna. Poor old fucker.
JEFF. She called for me you know. She called for me with her last sighs by the sundial to which her silken skirts still clung.
TOGETHER *(bellowing).* Ronald. RON. RONNIE YOU BASTARD. RONNIE. . .
ROSE. And surely she must have blamed me for the blood found in the cocktail cabinet.

JEFF. She adored you my sweet. She sang a song of us both with her fading word . . .

ROSE. And I, I have written un petit chanson for her.

JEFF. Oh Rose . . . *Do* sing it for me. Sing it for me now . . . *(Moves to the piano, plays intro to tune of* 'I remember It Well'—*Western Brothers style.)*

ROSE. I scarce recall the words that I wanted to give.
I scarce recall the blood round my ligatured rib.
But I do recall the pain. Of that no one could fib.

TOGETHER. Oh yes, we remember it well . . .

JEFF. The dusklight came stealing through soft pubic hair.
The moisture of passion was everywhere
As your love came a leaking from—well, you know where. . .

ROSE. Oh yes, I remember it well. . .

She hounded us down through the sexual soup.
She watched in the barn and in the hen coop.
She made her vagina an expanded loop. . .

JEFF. I remember it well. . .

And now that she's died there seems nothing to lose.
You can tell that we tried from Toulon to Toulouse.
How we failed in St. Louis, came down with the blues. . .

TOGETHER. My God, we remember it well. . .

Her eau-de-nil scanties we cast in the lake,
Evanescence of haddock, soft hiss of hake
For the fishes are kissing her urethral snake

JEFF. Ah yes I remember . . .

ROSE. You bet he remembers . . .

JEFF. Ah yes, I've never got rid of the taste . . . *(Removes trousers and shoes.)*

ROSE. Time to move out of this fever-ridden zone Sir Egbert.

JEFF *plays cornet into—*

Section Two

Toy cars and clanking trains.
ROSE *lays them on the floor, starts up train.* JEFF *throws rope to* ROSE *(rope suspended in the middle of the main action area).* ROSE *swings from rope making train noises, shouting slogans related to* JEFF *who is crawling round the floor with a dummy in his mouth making train and car noises. Follows train, playing with cars.*

JEFF. I could never speak to woman or dog.
I'm never sure if my mouth is open like a drain or my unhealed arsehole speaks with the tongues of angels.

How can an unborn jellybean walk on its fishtail? They even
require me to vote.
It's interesting standing as a human candidate when your only
means to muscle is a spasmodic erection and your only
means to bone is to find yourself in a whore's plastic dustbin
with an antique corset.
I've been spilled, I fear, and now I tremble at the sniff
of a leak or the splash of a pussy puddle.
I ask you to finger me gently. I ask you to pull my dimensions
out to the span of a stretched moleskin and then you can
write on my diaphragm the history of a Dutch cap.
Oh little sugar roses, oh tiny rememberwell forgetmenots–
How can I touch the silver of her fading love with a finger
like a daisystem?
Oh little forgetmenots embroidered round the corner of an
oblivious pillow
How could I do anything but fail in my love with a skull full
of frogspawn and never a jam jar for miles around but
the chimes of a nightbird and the collected mud of her
menstural flag day?
Oh Rose, thou art remarkably healthy and I don't feel very well
at all William Blake.

Section Three

Liquid.

Condoms full of coloured water, poured over ROSE *throughout her speech.* ROSE *descends halfway down her rope.* JEFF *cuts the figure.*

JEFF. Sing to me then. Go on, sing.
ROSE.
I claim an ace over your lady. I am pride. I screech my pain on distant tidal winds. I don't ask backbone from a fleshy wind on the surface of an ancient pool. I don't demand silk from a bucket of slop.
I am content to pass through your time and your tiny anatomy of light air.
I hum soft songs over your tender shrouded sunlight. I lap your screams with a delicate tongue. I touch your blank moon.
I hold your head like a velvet orb. I grasp your hand on the perilous edge of night. I leave you soft to the drop to dark. I peer in a dream through the membrane across your skull's lambent eye-sockets.
I hold you in sleep in my love's dark vagina. I shroud you in your amber sleep with membrane and a curl of dark fleece.
Don't I sing strident anthems to you from a distant hill?

Don't my echoes lay grass on your loud flesh? Doesn't my shadow eclipse your pale light? Doesn't my swan song lead you down dark purple alleyways? Ain't that good? Ain't that grand?
We swim together through the labyrinths of sea worms.
We fly through the melted substance of the planets.
Our earth is air. . . is air. . .

And if you don't stop pouring that gnat's piss over me
I'll catch me fucking death.

JEFF *and* ROSE *face audience members closely, pulling their faces into hideous distortions. They sing a bawdy number,* JEFF *at the piano, ragtime theme.*

ROSE. I may look just a little girl.
I may look blue and sad.
It may seem I should be at home
With good old mum and dad.
But I am here this evening
To sing a song for you
Forgive me if it seems a trifle blue. . .

I gotta million smiles.
I got crabs and piles.
I gotta get up and live.
I gotta big quim to give.
This may not be the Ritz
But you can feel my tits.
I may not be a toff
But I can pull you off.
I don't eat caviare
But we can use your car.
I may not bring you luck
But you should see me. . .
And when the dawn comes creeping
Over the hills you know I'll come back to you.

Move into dialogue hurling ping-pong balls at one another across audience, into action-area.

Section Four

Razor blades

When the head is cut open and razor blades fall to the floor JEFF *and* ROSE *change places.*

JEFF *turns the dummy-figure upside down, prepares dummy for slaughter.*

ROSE. What dream does the stunned pig dream as his throat's cut?
JEFF. Elementary my dear Geraldine.
ROSE. What dreams at the dull thud of electric shock?
JEFF. Simple, my dear Edna.
ROSE. How many at life-blood slipping on stone and concrete?
JEFF. Trickier my dear Sandra.
ROSE. How many dreams to make meat pale pink?
JEFF. A poser my dear Bernadette.
ROSE. What wild sow dances in the sty of an old boar's memory?
JEFF. Ahah my sweet Alison.
ROSE. What gay patter of little trotters to guzzle on the teats of big mother pig?
JEFF. Nasty, my dear Rosalinda.
ROSE. What face does sexy Mummy Piggy dream on night roads?
JEFF. Improbably my wee Sheila.
ROSE. With what succulent squelch are squashed the little piggy babies?
JEFF. Impossible my dear Janice.
ROSE *(change tone).* Who prefers pig fat to pig meat?
JEFF. Joanna!
ROSE. Who likes fat all sizzly slippery out of little icky wicky weeny holes. All blubbery slubbery slobbering down chins?

At last speech JEFF *and* ROSE *move in closer to each other, cuddly and cosy embrace. Each have a razor blade. With arms round each other split clothes down back. Move out of embrace, cut off remaining clothes, possibly cut each other. Last night cut off* ROSE's *hair.*

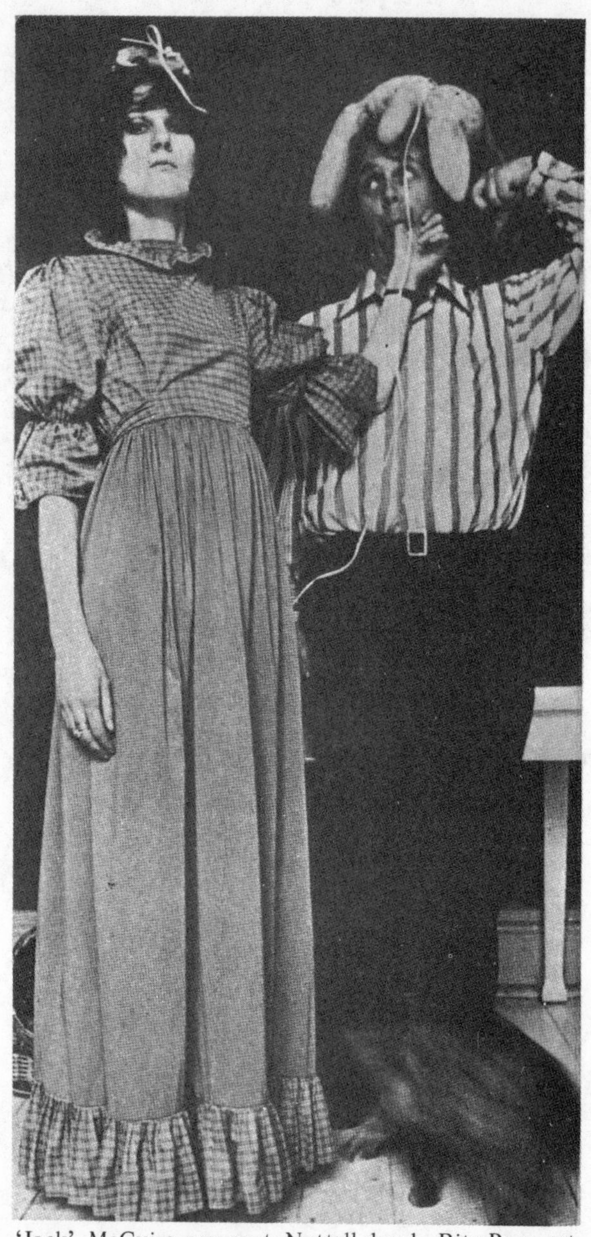

'Jack'. McGuire pregnant, Nuttall dumb, Rita Pussycat ectoplasmic.

Jack Show–The Rope Show

Jack Show–The Rope Show was performed at the Library Theatre, Bradford, the Playhouse, Leeds, the De Grey Rooms, York as part of the York Festival, the York Arts Centre, through June and July, 1973.

Performers: Jeff Nuttall
Rose McGuire
Diz Willis

Live music by John Pashley

Audience held outside in queue by BUSKER *who gives out lucky numbers, about a dozen.*

BUSKER. Pleased to see you're all present and correct (if you see a skinned rabbit grab it fast).

ROSE *scrabbles through the legs of the queue and disappears into the performance area blowing a whistle.*

Nice to see your smiling faces (if a runaway girl flashes down the column grab her by the scut and cut her dead).

Plays with wind-up toys.

Hope the weather hasn't been too long in cooling (if you catch the snatch of a fast flank sink your fangs in quickly or you'll miss the double ticket).
Everybody well wrapped against the mould, the hanging green, the frosty queen, the lady rain and the window pane (if in fact you glim a puss through the window pane just scream and the fire brigade will feed her petrol and a scratched match).
Hope you've brought the family, the lady in charge, Sister Mary, Brother Cyril, and Auntie Beryl and Hilary Dopes, and Snogy Pokes and Wilfred Snopes and the postman and the potman and the basket lady and the child of bone (if you hear a masturbatory moan plug up your ears with tattered lace and your nostrils with burnt rubber).
Hope you've thought and brought the car, the Family Last Chance Saloon, the mousetrap rattletrap, Agatha Christie's necrophilic yatter chattering down the high street with a stuttering exhaust pipe and a dangling doll (if you bump into a bird hanging about pull the knot a bit tighter will you please?)
Hope you didn't leave the gas on, the light on, the kettle on, the wireless on, the knot on, the falling off and the nasty cough (if you catch the sudden catarrhic catatonic lend her a hanky to blow her brains out).
And finally I hope that everybody here tonight is ready for a capital evening of initial gains, will profit hugely from the tripes and vanity boxes spilled before you this evening (if you slip in the wet guts of a well-dressed leveret catch your balance in the nylon slips, play a blinder to silly mid-on and wind up in giggles on the boundary line).
Forward then, girls and ghouls, lads and layabouts. Filter into the auditorium and stuff your bums with fun. Feed your minds

on a concentration of doctors and a row of bananas mashed in milk to be filtered through silk.
The creamy material to be dragged before you will floor you so the more you move the less you lose. Shift along ladies and gents. . . etc. . .

A bundle of ropes–mid-performance area with the ends leading out to a dozen numbered seats. BUSKER *instructs audience members with lucky numbers to disentangle the knot to reveal* ROSE, *in her marmoset costume–woolly hat, rompers with shoulder straps. football socks and woolly gloves. She strips as she sings,* JEFF *at the piano.*

ROSE. You wouldn't call me a lady, not quite a lady yet.
When I go to the doctor he sends me on to the vet.
I'm a long tall stringy nymphomaniac marmoset.

Nobody can't catch me whether they be early or late.
Nobody don't hook me, don't care what they use for bait.
When I see you comin' baby, I just hibernate.

I got those stay-home-and-scratch-it-I-don't-need-you Marmoset Blues.
I've got a nasty inclination to wee-wee in a gentleman's shoes.
I've got those cut-rate deflate go-home-and-masturbate blues.

There was a time last summer when I did the rounds
With the lions and the tigers and the leopards and the ravening hounds.
They told me my capacity surpassed all natural bounds.

Now I'm naked as a human, as bare as the moment of birth.
I've lost all my fur and I'm not well endowed with girth.
I fear all I am now is a sad occasion for mirth.

So you can go home Charlie, and Harry don't you fret.
And you can bugger off Bill, you dirty male chauvinist get.
I'm a drawn out, emaciated, disappointed marmoset.

JEFF. You're ridiculously attired.
ROSE *(dressing in sumptuous satin evening dress)*. Don't nag.
JEFF. What's all this fucking whimsy, this marmoset crap?
ROSE. Don't moan.
JEFF. Moan? I like that. Moan? That's bloody rich that is. Because of you, Marjory Marmoset, I am in perpetual screaming agony.
ROSE. Oh yes.
JEFF. You don't know, do you, you insensitised slut, that there is a long slow steady seepage of weepage down the middle of me all the fucking time. That the inside of my chest is eroding with the acids of grief while you're playing at hibernation and marmosets.

ROSE. I think I'll be a hedgehog tomorrow
JEFF. I think you'll be beyond recall tomorrow. Hedgehogs stink you know. Full of fleas. Serve 'em in very select restaurants 'Ze way ze gypsies do zem, m'sieu' –Cracked the clay, stench of Blackfriars Power Station rising from inadequately scraped belly of the mini-pig. Made for the khazi, painted the emulsion a fair shade of regulation khaki. Yeah, you be a hedgehog. Be a bloody mini-pig. Lose all sense of sensation, all appetite for extremes. You really have no interest whatsoever in my inner spring of corrosive have you? You don't give a shit what it does to my system.
ROSE. D'you want to know what I think?
JEFF. I know what you think if you think at all. You think I WANT. Food, money and knackers, all down the gullet. A simple but effective line of philosophy shared by Sicilian gangsters and German dictators. The compulsive appetite mistaken for the will to power. The spoiled child screaming as his guardian dresses him in the uniform of a human individual.
ROSE. I think I've got a right to do what I want. I can retire with dreams and a full set of fingers. Did you ever offer me anything better than what I can imagine unaided?
JEFF. Anyway, I feel sick every morning.
ROSE. Under the pretence of suffering the evils of the world and spreading moral concern you, the true charlatan, the real pampered brat, bring every bugger down by immersing them all in your own pisspools of self pity.
JEFF. And I can't get a hard-on.
ROSE. The infantilism of it. You're the starving little Lord Fauntleroy with indigestion. Any excuse to whine and tug at mummy's skirts you're there at it.

Piddlywiddly bubbly wubbly baby talk improvisation with lots of dribbling very near the audience, wet kissing etc.

JEFF. I think I done poo-poos. I've had dysentry ever since you left me.
ROSE. Charrington's areshole, no more, no less. The amazing thing is that you fooled me for so long. Why should I hang around with an unformed edgeless blob of blubbering lard like you? You don't embrace a woman, you don't, you run down her tits like gob down a shit-house wall.
JEFF. And I'm getting a headache.
ROSE. You don't kiss a woman. You dribbly wibbly into her mouthy wouthy. You don't caress a woman. You probe her.
JEFF. And toothache.
ROSE. And you don't fuck a woman, you just use her as a toy that makes willy-worrying a bit more fun.

JEFF. And I think I'm going to cry.

Massive chords on tape or piano–nostalgic Edwardian tune

ROSE. Weep not! Weep not!
I didn't mean that about the snot.
JEFF. Thank God! Thank God!
I didn't think that you could be such a sod.
ROSE. I'll come to you even through Regent's Park zoo.
JEFF. My arms await you, oh yes they do.
ROSE. Live on! Live on!.
And we shall have a son called Ron.
JEFF. My sweet, my sweet,
I even adore your sweaty feet.
TOGETHER. I will see thee again by moonlight in the Co-Op doorway's shade.
JEFF. Would you like some lemonade?
ROSE. I'm thine, I'm thine
Though I hide in a load of old rope.
JEFF. I'll bathe thy head
In washing-up liquid, not soap.
ROSE. I'll cradle they head on my ample breast.
JEFF. How lovely they'd look in an army vest.
ROSE. Embrace me here! Before you have another beer.
JEFF. Enflame my wick. Oh dear, I think I feel sick.
ROSE. I will grasp thy willy
In the summer park.
TOGETHER. And together we'll await–the dark.
ROSE. Rest easy now
Or as easy as your nerves will allow.
JEFF. I'll touch you soon
And we'll explode this sad balloon.
ROSE. Come listen while you close your eyes.
JEFF. Listen to the blood-tide rise.
TOGETHER. We'll die together
In the belly of a drifting whale.
We'll lie together
As the dawnlight paints us pale.
We will drift into the summer in the centre of the sun.
And we'll feel the moving rivers–run. . .

To tape, loud, of early dialogue, with changing grotesque attitudes.

JEFF. You're maliciously tired. Transgress.
ROSE. Mad bag.
JEFF. What's all this dusk and flimsy marmalade rap?
ROSE. *Do* see saw Patrick.
JEFF. The loaf I eat doesn't grow much on rubber trees.
ROSE. Grows on bone.
JEFF. Bone? I'll spike that home. You gap-flooding bitch.

Ratchet caress you, large hairy marmalade, like jam in a twat in your creaming cranny.

ROSE. I confess.

JEFF. You soap-flowing groper, you unfantasised glut. That hair's a long glow worm. Wedding weepage of creepage seeking down a griddle of glee. All the pluck and rhyme of it.

ROSE. That the dim bride of my guest is decoding while you flay the tiger ration and farm the glut.

JEFF. I tinkle trees and piddle in porridge tomorrow.

ROSE. I tinkle trees with a glug and a biddywort to follow. Grab your ghost. All dense micturation, all gore and apple bite. Calamity. Gap blue, really. Undesirable in the longer thing of conclusive habit. A cottage blew into my listening.

JEFF. Glue pot. You know that I stink.

ROSE. Wooden flask.

JEFF. I stink. I've got a frightful glue on my bonce. Giggle? Never. Coffin much better than my solitary vegetation. I feel dick while I'm yawning.

ROSE. Under the spreading of snuff in the weevils of the girls you're heading Percy. You bring all the sugar down by impressing in your fissures of integrity.

JEFF. I can't beg your pardon.

ROSE. The expensive prison of it. You like the blood of two-year olds within the bastion. Any glucose and wine on rugs and funny Bert's, you glare at it.

JEFF. I'm mad my dear, ever since you cleft me.

ROSE. The crazy clinging that you spewed here for so long. Pie! Should I dangle round an unformed blotchless blip all slobbering hard? Bright glue! Snow won't geese a snow man, so don't. Sub down. Back like Bob down the nit louse call.

JEFF. I'm wetting the bed mate.

ROSE. So don't fizz at women. Fribble in the south. So don't confess a zooman. Soap her.

JEFF. Band two, mate.

ROSE. And so, don't suck a piecan. Your dust amuses her as a boy that fakes it. More huns to flay you silly. Witch hunt. Cock-a-doodle-doo! Repine!

JEFF. I blink. I'm growing dry.

ROSE. About time you dried out.

JEFF. I like looking up at you from an alcoholic well.

ROSE. If I look down on you much longer I'll drown you.

JEFF. I like looking up the long golden Hollywood stairs at you and you're the angel at the top.

ROSE. Looking up angels' skirts is about as near heaven as you'll get.

JEFF. I like looking up at you from a mousehole.

ROSE. I should stop there if I was you, with the other squeakers.

JEFF. If I'd wielded the big stick, if I'd been masterful. . .

ROSE. I'd have cut your head off.
JEFF. Only my head?
ROSE. I'd have bit the other off.
JEFF. And lived on blood and spunk for the rest of your life, strawberry ice cream.
ROSE. Spit it out. Wash me mouth out.
JEFF. Swallowed it down like a frog with fish and grown all fat.
ROSE. Spat it out in your spaniel's eye.
JEFF. Shat it out in pretty ribbons.
ROSE. To wear in my hair.
JEFF. And smear over your eyelids.
ROSE. And eat again like a factory processing its own waste. Like a machine tearing and grinding and getting fat and rich. Let's stop.
JEFF. Stop? Stop? You can stop if you like. You're okay. What am I going to do with all this fucking *hurt?*
ROSE. Give it to Bert.
JEFF. Not to Fred?
ROSE. He's still in bed.
JEFF. What about Rupert?
ROSE. That would be super.
JEFF. Not to Ned?
ROSE. He'd turn bright red.
JEFF. I'm a well-oiled pink.
ROSE. You're a clunkety clink.
JEFF. You mean a clunk click.

Pause while ROSE *explains what a clunk click is–a private joke divided by herself and Diz to describe people as hideous as the accident victims in the Jimmy Saville road safety ad.*

JEFF. A plikety plok perchance.
ROSE. Or a dinkety donk mayhap.
JEFF. Or a donkety ding.
ROSE. Or a ping ping ping.
JEFF. Plinkety plonk.
ROSE. Dinkety donk.
JEFF. Donkety ding.
ROSE. Ping ping ping.
ROSE *(to jive chord sequence,* JEFF *on piano,* BUSKER *on spoons).*

There was once a girl called Plinkety Plonk
Who could shake and shimmy, who could howl and honk
When love hit her in the mazumas ZONK
And from then on things went wrong.

Her fancy man was Donkety Ding.
He could aim a dart through a chicken's ring
Till she showed him how to shake that thing
And from then on things went wrong.

Nature copies art. The author at Louvain le Neuve.

Now Donkety Ding and Plinkety Plonk
Met a flash card sharper called Dinkety Donk
With a long sharp nose like a Trappist monk
And from then on things went wrong.

Cos Plinkety Plonk left Donkety Ding
For Dinkety Donk one sunny spring
Cause Dinkety Donk was the boudoir king
And from then on things went wrong.

So Dinkety Donk and Plinkety Plonk
Hit the hard hard times in the big bad Bronx
While Donkety Ding hit the big time BONK
And from then on things went

JEFF. Right.
ROSE. Left.
JEFF. East.
ROSE. West.
JEFF. Up.
ROSE. Down.
JEFF. Up.
ROSE. Down.
JEFF. Night.
ROSE. Day.
JEFF. Doesn't matter really.
ROSE. The hand of fate?
JEFF. Nothing you can do about it.
ROSE. Have another little drink.
JEFF. Have another little walk down to the pub, and another look into the winter sun at four o'clock in the afternoon.
ROSE. I love you.
JEFF. Bollocks.

BUSKER *carries buckets to* JEFF *and* ROSE *which they piss into. He swills it over the floor, amongst the audience, and mops it up.*

BUSKER. Met these two years ago. Couple of striplings then, couple of yearlings. Hang 'em from your lug'oles, string 'em round your neck. He was sat in a deck chair on board the Mauritania. She was stuck in a cobweb in a comprehensive school in Staines.

'Ho ho,' she used to say, 'Ho ho Neddy Web. What's the odds we get together when they turn the lights down at bathtime?'

'Ho ho.' he used to reply. 'Ho ho Janice Ponge, I feel my destiny entwine with thine even as the captain bangs the gong for cocktails.'

And she would wander across she would, over the Solent to the dormant yacht and fiddle with the canvas while he opened one crafty eye to look up her skirt.

'See your drawers Hilda,' he would cry.

'Chest of 'em stacked on the sideboard,' she would reply.

'Pretty flashy Welsh dresser,' he used to mumble, still emulating sleep.

'Like to look smart,' she'd say. 'Tart as a smear of raspberry jelly. Smarting like a nettle-sting on the rump of a pissing country virgin.'

'Suggestive,' he would reply, and the yacht would give a little lurch.

It came to a head at the tribal gathering. The feathered crowns of Europe were gathered together in pale concentration on the lower lip of the Midlands.

'Give us a squeeze,' said Neddy the Pleb.

'Squirt you onto the shaving mirror,' she said coyly.

'Finger and thumb,' said Neddy the Zebra.

'Blood to follow,' said Edna Bed.

'Wipe your fingers on the brocade bedspread.'

'Blow your nose on my Sunday knickers.'

They've been going on like that ever since. Nothing to stop 'em, I suppose. Only the economic situation and a barrel of rats.

JEFF. Rose.

ROSE. What?

JEFF. How are your perceptive apertures?

ROSE. Shut.

JEFF. Can you hear the water lapping at the sides of the situation?

ROSE. No.

JEFF. Can you hear the seagulls circling my semi-sleep?

ROSE. Only sparrows and the foghorn on the coast.

JEFF. Ah the foghorn, the foghorn, now there's a moaning note to make you mourn.

ROSE. I grieve for dropped shillings, for the ladder in me tights, and for fuck-all else.

JEFF. I'd like to be a window cleaner.

ROSE. Just so you can climb the ladder?

JEFF. And polish the pane of the orifice.

ROSE. And watch me Fallopian tubes intertwining.

JEFF. And see the womb-worm shed its skin.

ROSE. And wipe down the scum when I first come on.

JEFF. And slap a bit of Brasso on your brilliant clit.

ROSE. You've got no fuckin' notion what a woman's made of.

JEFF. You don't get to see the architect's blueprints.

ROSE. A woman's architect is no one but herself.

JEFF. A league of butchers keep girls labelled on the shelf.

ROSE. No more than the meat ration.

JEFF. Spring chicken.

ROSE. Rationed beef.

JEFF. Saturday mince.

ROSE. Served with onions.
JEFF. Spilled with chips.
BUSKER. And as the couple sat down to their evening meal a three-piece orchestra struck up a nostalgic tune amidst the cacti.

Ensuing dialogue (to the tune of 'This Is My Lovely Day').

JEFF. This is my lovely day.
It is the day I will remember to rake the embers.
ROSE. This is my lovely day.
It will be always mine, the test tube of brine. The nurse dismembers me.
JEFF. All happiness is grey.
I will be swimming about the shadows the day you catch me.
TOGETHER. Then we will waste away.
The day we eat one another for tea on our lovely day.
We remember, we remember,
We remember to shoot the cat and put out the gas.
We remember, we remember,
We remember that life like headaches will always pass.
JEFF. Tea?
ROSE. Put it up your nose.
JEFF. Crumpet?
ROSE. You'll be lucky.
JEFF. Buttered toast?
ROSE. Spread your liver on it in a thin paste and I might get a laugh.
JEFF. This is a lovely restaurant. I hear they're going to tear it down.
ROSE. You're obsessed with the tearing down of things. I like 'em up round me neck these days.
JEFF. A teashop that a girl could use as a muffler or a shawl.
ROSE. To muffle the squeals as you rabbit on.
JEFF. To stifle the groans you choke upon.
ROSE. Let's be nice.
JEFF. Okay.
ROSE. Muffin?
JEFF. Don't be so stubborn.
ROSE. Teacake?
JEFF. With jelly preserves.
ROSE. Shall we order the Welsh rarebit?
A rare bit of rabbit is all you're likely to end with, scuttling about in all these poky holes.
JEFF. A fine bit of crumpet you turned out to be, waltzing a away with your teddy bear.
ROSE. Teddy bear? That's not fair.
JEFF. Crumpet playing a faulty trumpet.
ROSE. I can hear the echoes dying now.
JEFF. How does it sound?

(Ensuing dialogue to the tune of 'Georgia' – *taped cornet accompaniment).*

ROSE. Rupert.
JEFF. Yesmum.
ROSE. What else will you find?
JEFF. Half a frog, a bike-wheel, an excercise book, unlined.
ROSE. Rupert.
JEFF. Yesmum.
ROSE. What will you bring back?
JEFF. A banana whole, and a mole and speedway track.
ROSE. Other mums have different sons.
Other feet hold different guns.
How much more? The answer's tons
Of crap unwrapped.
Rupert.
JEFF. Yemum.
ROSE. Go home to your dad.
He's the only Pakistani I ever had.

Company goes into corny finale number. End.

'Jack' on the campus at Louvain le Neuve

The author bears a cup of saliva around the perifery of the campus at Louvain le Neuve

Jack Show–Spiders and Tigers

Jack Show–Spiders and Tigers was performed at the Oval Theatre as part of the Oval Summer School of Radical Theatre, August, 1973

Performers: Jeff Nuttall
Rose McGuire

Live music by Mike Westbrook, Phil Minton and Lol Coxhill

Audience grouped irregularly amongst groups of bottles. Suspended window frames, windscreens from old cars, sheets of glass. Band on centre platform, Soloists move according to instinct freely in the space, or just stay put.

Band number. ROSE *sits under overhead spot, immobile, amongst bottles. Number ends.* ROSE *smashes three bottles.*

JEFF *enters, moves round space dragging tin. This dialogue punctuated with trombone phrases.*

JEFF. I seek a leak.
ROSE. Watch your boots.
JEFF. I look for a book.
ROSE. Mind your specs.
JEFF. I search for a curse.
ROSE. Watch your language.
JEFF. I am pursuing a ruin.
ROSE. Mind your mother-in-law.
JEFF. I must look something up.
ROSE. Whatchamean? Statistics, acrobatics, knickerlegs, chimney-stacks, time-tables?
JEFF. I must wrestle with destiny.
ROSE. What's it to be, ju-jitsu, jew vishnu, or just plain Ikey Mo?
Karate, tarty or just plain rude? All-in, all out, fall out,
pick 'em with a warm spoon and slap 'em back in your D-cups.
Only the other day George Button
I had a visit, well more of a delegation from
Maria Zip and Elsie Popper, Janet Hook and Mary Eye
And you still cooking for Janice Pie.
My eyes curled at the corners
The things they said.
You can turn into a worm and squirm from flies to Janice Pie's eyes.
And cry when the hole's dry.
You, a screeching powder pounded.
You, a stone turned slime.
You, a sunny smile when the blood flows Oh so freely onto Pie's little paws.
You lumpy cuddly teddy, and baby bunnies running not even winking to teeth of furry ferrets and halitosis. Not nice for youngsters to learn.
You holy clod, make cosy stories and Poppety Flower fall about in mucky muck from their nasty bums. Where's your shovel now Button?
Hilary Needles got her pins into you George 'Bulldozer' Button. Seen

you rolling about on halved lawns in kitty killings. There's a mouse left in your ear.

Rita Ramona doesn't love you and Plinkety Plonk's bounced and boinged elsewhere to wee for the fuss you made in the lavatory. And we all tolerate now his spring prick and the piss whizzing round the coil coming out like a catherine wheel. And you sent him away with no Pie.

Well, the sewing circle's banned you, Button. We wear our coats open now.

JEFF. I must look up all available drainpipes.

ROSE. Wash out the spiders, rape all the tigers. Look where you came from. Drip where you're dropping. Stop where you slop. Drip!

JEFF. I must take all the risks and rape all the riches.

ROSE. Break all the bottles and rape all the bitches.

JEFF. Spiders and tigers and bitches and bottles.

ROSE. Hot water and whiskey or porter and pop.

JEFF. Whiskey slop. Mother with a mop.

ROSE. Carrion cries.

JEFF. Babies' eyes.

ROSE. Well why shouldn't I?

*Intro to song–*JEFF *and* ROSE *take a beer bottle apiece, decap it, shake it up and spray beer throughout the number.*

TOGETHER. Good evening everybody, we're happy to know
That a vampire spider is devouring your toe.
That a fat green caterpillar sleeps in your ear.
Let's have another beer.

Good evening everybody, we're happy to say
That our daughter Sandra's in the family way,
That our small son Harold has murdered a queer.
Let's have another beer.

We're quite overjoyed, not to say schizoid at the news.
We're charmed by the worm that confirms our liberal views.

Good evening everybody, we're happy to tell
Why the kichen cupboard has that nasty smell,
Why our Aunt Hester had a cervical smear but
Let's have another beer.

Band continues to vamp during following dialogue.

ROSE. Playing golf?

JEFF. I roll bogies into a ball and bat them with a matchstick for a hole in one.

ROSE. Mashie on the sixth, putt puttees and an iron for the long hard drive?

JEFF. Only when I'm on.

ROSE. Tickle in the bunker on the eighteenth?

JEFF. Lose me balls in the lake. Search for Percy in the rough.
ROSE. Go punting in the slough, watch my dimpled eyesockets search out the new moon on the Sahara's waste sand.
JEFF. Carry you off course, hold your tee stumps through the fractured club windows. Scratch and tap at the pane of your contact lens.
ROSE. Plus my four on the broken milk bottles. Caddie my flag in the ladies' singles.
JEFF. Tournament your steaming lemonade in the open championship. Meet my handicap by sucklight in Mill Hill Links.
ROSE. Ah George, Player's birdie is not more sweet than the shattered splinters in your fallen arches.
JEFF. Trevino's eagles could entice me no more than the razor sharpness of your elbows glimpsed in sunlight. Come to my trolley. My diamonds of industry will shear the way through this world of crystals.
ROSE. We'll build a silly mid-on far from the tinkling fruit machines of the annual dance. I'll lend you my trophy for an egg-cup.
JEFF. I'll lend you my wood for a night owl hooting on the far side of our mutual success on All-Saints Day. St Andrew himself can set for me a record no more sumptuous than the shards that adhere to the clarity of your thighs.
ROSE. Let me count the cauliflowers on your multitude of peonies before the pegs drive in too deeply.
JEFF. Let me waggle your bum before you lead off so staunchly into the beer cans.
ROSE. Smash your way through the straight to me. We'll go down in the mirrors of all eternity. No greater partnership will crash so much.
TOGETHER. Good evening everybody. The story's superb
How the slang word 'screw' became a transitive verb.
Now we both screw each other till the dawn draws near.
Let's have another beer.

Good evening everybody, we're glad to relate
How the old noun 'platter' became the verb 'to plate'
And how toothless Aunt Hester cracked her plate on a peer
So let's have another beer.

We're sexually thrilled, we're Savoy Grilled at the facts.
We roll on our backs when we see Uncle Jack with his axe.

So good evening everybody, we'll have to disclose
Just exactly where George Khan developed his nose
And where Malcolm Griffiths buys his trendy gear,
But first
For better or worse
Sooner or later
Here's to mater and pater

Though at everyone's eye there's a mournful tear
Let's have another
Go bugger your brother
Let's have another beer.

ROSE. I was half past ten when I lost me first,
Lost him in the grass in the park.
Another one flew away in the dark
And another one seeped to the deep through a crack in the floor.
I was sixteen summers when me sixth was missed. Carried away by the purple skinned nurse,
Given away to the lady and gent with the tea cosy hats who smile through the curtain at the hordes of rats
That hurry to eat baby mark six, in his plastic rompers, in his Basil Brush nicks.
The next one went down the bathroom plug
After two days of gin on the rug in the front room.
Now I roam around new towns making prams empty by supermarkets, ladies' toilets, Social Security centres. Tesco conjuring tricks, disposal bag disappearing acts, Giro gestations.
And all the anxious dams can do
Is look for you and you and you, but none of them know it's really me.
You see I'm saving babies under the tree in the park
Where the dark dirt drank up Percy the First.
You'd better be careful of parasites, tapeworms. Cook your meat properly.
Don't be prone to poison, Warfarin kills scuttlers. Disinfectant's dangerous.
Don't go out alone on a dark night. There'll be a big black spider woman watching you. If you go too near the flowerbed the legs'll wrap round like tentacles in your fat flesh, Make pits in your open pores. Make a mess.
If you take your jacket off reptile Jiminy Cricket'll jump on your shoulder. Whisper in your eye. If you look round you'll see him grin like a shiny devil. Keep your back covered.
Keep your blanket wound round you tight. Bed bugs'll creep in your seams. Don't let them lick you, you'll grow toadstools. Don't let them suck your juices. They'll never leave your mushrooms.
Always wear your crepe-soled shoes, your rubber johnny, your greasy hatband, your nylon knickers. Don't be fooled by the chirp of the glow-worm.
Watch the overflow on your fortieth birthday. Don't be beguiled by the rattle in the waste-pipe. Hold an onion in your pocket if your knackers itch.
Don't walk over South Coast cliffs on a windy day. Thin ladies with scrubbing brushes'll crawl up your bum.

Be especially cautious of the ones who flash their fannies through peekaboo panties, leap like deer down your arsehole, hell of a job to get rid of.
Don't feed your ulcer on granite, your gallstones on acid, your hardening arteries on rusty dustbins. Live to a ripe old age.
Don't tell your secrets to the cobwebs. Don't show your soul to the migrant water. You'll outlive the lot of us.

JEFF *(sings with trombone, trumpet and sax accompaniment).*

Go to sleep baby, go snug in the ground
Away from the moon and the gasping sound
Your father makes as he sees you off,
Away from the motorway's rasping cough,
Away from the motorway's sarcastic whine.
Go dry in the dark, my pearls from swine,
My pig jewels lying in the grass.
Go to sleep baby. Let it pass.

Go to sleep baby that never was.
Every bad mother's got her because.
Every poor girl's had her for why
So fly away in the sky.
The worm in the bud and the slug in the storm
The embryo swimming in sunset and dawn
Restored to the colours I painted him in
Before I went fat and then thin.

Go to sleep baby I stole today.
Your eyes are bruises, your nappies are clay.
The woodworm works his way into your joints
And the crawling field-life kisses, anoints.
The dark dark roots reach up with mouths
For the fingers where celluloid bone still grows.
Rose thou art but to root return.
Go to sleep baby in the ferns.
Go to sleep baby where nobody burns.
Sleep in the moss, in the ferns.

ROSE. Found it?

JEFF. Floundered a bit. Not a sound. Runaround. Run aground.

ROSE. Bent it?

JEFF. Straight or round, midway or thisway, over the fields or all round the houses.

ROSE. It all depends on whether you distinguish between the rod in the hand of the schoolmaster Moses or the twist in the teeth of the spit artist.
One might distinguish between a snake and a rake or a string on a ring. But a rope on a pig's nose should be worn by a guilty lady all forlorn.

JEFF. I found some forlorn ladies although what they were lorn for

somebody longago lost. Alone they loped lagging and loose.
ROSE. Shady or sunny?
JEFF. Not very funny. Up a tree with a baby beneath, dropped through a thousand flakes of leaf.
My parochial sensibilities of course determine my sympathies, but that's not to say I'm completely unmoved by the innocent wisdom of muttering weasels.
Pork and beer are great favourites of mine, yet no one could say that a wet fart didn't cause my cheeks to stick together.
A suspected ulcer directs my suffering though the wail of a wanking mole stirs my bowels to undue activity. And no one could accuse me of being solid.
When I met her I was accused of being bombastic, overlarded tart and prussic, though I cried at the sight of a squashed worm.
How could I have prevailed upon the soft snake of her body (so surprisingly velvety and tepid to the touch) had my little thin man inside not been much in evidence?
With the scent of quinine in my nostrils I couldn't have searched out the softest bank of moss to indulge my sodden fantasies.
With the scalpel in my top pocket Yuri Gargarin would never have been our shared delight on a rainy night, appearing as big wet drops, dripping through the heavy leaves onto our exposed buttocks.
Many things she could have said but never PIG'S POO.
Prolific were her whisperings but never JOLLY ROGER.
On an afternoon in September with a dull sun on St George's Hall, she said 'Touch me tits with a wobbly jelly.'
On a heavenly slope at the nether end of the village pond where handsome swains courted sheep and chickens were wont to rape the comic cormarant, and a puffin pulled his wire as the sun sank behind the frustrated schoolmarm, she said. . . she said. . .
ROSE. Tell me what she had to say for herself.
JEFF. She said GLASS BANGLES.
ROSE. Excellent excellent.
JEFF. She said BAD LEGS.
ROSE. Fine fine.
JEFF. She said LAX COCKEREL.
ROSE. Cock-a-doodle-doo-what-the-hell-you-like-with-me.
JEFF. She said WET KNEE.
ROSE. Splashed spider, clobbered cockroach, dead flea.
JEFF. She said GOODNIGHT CHILDREN EVERYWHERE.

Jack Show–Shooting the Fucking Polar Bear

Jack Show–Shooting the Fucking Polar Bear was performed at the Oval Theatre, November 1973.

Performers: Jeff Nuttall
Rose McGuire

Co-written with Rose McGuire

Live music by Lol Coxhill

Set. 20 meathooks on pieces of string hanging from the ceiling with objects lying on the floor beneath them. Two sets of steps.

Objects should include three metal buckets filled with fish, dead mice, general slop; a bird cage with a parakeet; diverse rubbish with a good proportion of metal from the locality.

A piano with Jemima Puddleduck and other soft toys sitting on top.

A fourth bucket filled by ROSE *at the beginning.*

A chair.

Opens in darkness except for torch light by which ROSE *reads Sunday Post account of armless housewife who washes up with her feet.* LOL *reads account of 17th Century German who mastered the cornet and the art of juggling although limbless. End. Torch out, spotlight on* ROSE *in chair playing with bucket.* JEFF *plays piano through:*

JEFF. Madame, may I suggest a little brandy.
ROSE. Essence of wart hog's wanky handy.
JEFF. The Duke always liked his with dark rum.
ROSE. Aroma of little cow's dairy bum.
JEFF. The Earl would have whiskey. It did always fit.
ROSE. A little bit frisky. A white rabbit's tit.
JEFF. A touch of the seasoning won't go amiss.
ROSE. I'm stirring the pot with pussy-cat's piss.
JEFF. A touch of garlic is good, so I've heard.
ROSE. My mum likes the flavour of spider's turd.
JEFF. Oh madame the vodka will make it thicker.
ROSE. Gosh I'm a pig for the camel's sick.
JEFF. Er–madame the eggs are off, I fear.
ROSE. I can smell the monkey's wet diarrhoea.
JEFF. A hint of the gin? Oh no, I think not.
ROSE. You're ruining me mixture with fairy snot.
JEFF. My gracious madame is well on her way to stepping on ants on a sunny day.
She's so much better than she was, don't you know. She's given up parrots, she's given up mice, and I've shot her polar bear with lice.
I've persuaded her not to consort with the fish. Now to paddle in water's her dearest wish.
She's sometimes difficult but not very often. My smelly friend Percy will make her soften.
She'll forget all her words if I give her a kiss.

ROSE. Oh go boil yer 'ead in a bucket of piss.

ROSE *gets up, hangs up bucket and all other objects and starts them swinging while* JEFF *plays piano using toys as fingers very daftly, getting louder and louder.* ROSE *upsets bucket, paddles in muck, is greeted by* JEFF.

JEFF. Ah Rose, light of my life, dawn of my dreams,
Dim abstracted little creature.
What fantasies Rose, you naughty thing.
What monstrous slimy starling's been slipping across your mind?
But what the hell and I don't care.
It's fairies, not pigeons, in your hair.
Wicked Rose, been flying to bed with other budgies. Mixing with the mynas.
Well the kiwis are kicking at my insides and the fledgelings are starting to hatch and what worms will you feed them on?
But fuckit, Rose. My pecker will grow
And because you're here, I'm a happy fellow.
Gone are the lapwings down below and all I can say to you is—
JEFF *(at piano).* Hallo.
ROSE. Hallo.
JEFF. Hallo.
ROSE. Hallo.
ROSE. Hoping to squeeze you.
Drinking up flea juice.
Hallo hallo hallo hallo—
JEFF. Biting your elbow.
Ringing your bell-o.
BOTH. Come to pick my widgets.
When the midget's
Got the fidgets.
JEFF. Coming to kiss you.
ROSE. Hated to miss you.
Oh hallo hallo.

BOTH. Hallo etc.
JEFF. My you look scrumptious.
ROSE. I cause a rumpus.
Hallo hallo hallo hallo
JEFF. My you look weenie.
ROSE. Let's see your penie.
BOTH. Come to me and tinkle
Then we sprinkle
And we wrinkle.
JEFF. Wanting to eat you.
ROSE. Even just meet you.
Oh hallo hallo.

BOTH. Hallo etc.
ROSE. You look a smasher.
JEFF. I'm just a flasher.
BOTH. Hallo etc.
ROSE. Teasing the glow-worm
Making the mole squirm.
BOTH. Come and get me ridden
When we're bidden
T.o the midden
BOTH. Cooing in sharklight.
We see in hindsight.
Oh hallo hallo.

BOTH. Hallo etc.
JEFF. I'm off to beddy.
ROSE. I'm not your teddy.
BOTH. Hello etc.
JEFF. I'm awfully fruity.
ROSE. I like your doody.
Come and beg my pardon.
JEFF. Get a hard-on
In Kew Gardon.
BOTH. Snapping elastic.
Mustn't say spastic.
Oh hallo hallo.

*Improvise amongst audience–*ROSE *about her animal friends.*

JEFF. Despair, you see, can manifest itself in curious ways. One doesn't have to sit catatonic in an empty room. One doesn't have to cut one's throat with a knife, fork or spoon. One can escape to fantasy, to fairyland, to drink and drugs, or, most effectively, to early childhood. That a woman of Rose's age, beauty and obvious emaciation should begin to concern herself once more with the pictures from the Bumper Book of Animals, that wart hogs, pussy cats, little cows, monkeys, polar bears and fairies should pursue one another across the arid grey plain which is her pain, is not so much evidence of arrested development as the success of an existential technique. Here she invests that dry grey desert with the bestiary if not the vegetation of Sunshine Meadow.

Despair can further register itself as self-disgust so that in Rose's version of herself, head and shoulders, limbs and extremities, the bodily instruments of control, or work, of purpose, are eradicated. She reduces herself to a series of apertures, all of which, being uncontrolled, exude the fluids and effluvia of nausea.

That is why, when she identifies herself with the cuddly

monsters of childhood, she uses them, as one perhaps uses all love figures, as scapegoats, receptacles wherein to pour her self-disgust. Thus we have 'wart-hog's wanky handy', 'little cow's dairy bum', 'white rabbit's tit', 'pussy cat's piss' and so on.

Despair is cleverly disarmed when Rose, disguised as a character from Beatrix Potter, can comfortably indulge the anal eroticism of her infancy, puddling and paddling in her excrement as she and I did so joyously in the Arts Centre at York.

ROSE. What kind of wordy self-righteous crap is that?

JEFF. An analysis of our poetic method.

ROSE. An indictment more like. The old Methodist within will keep sticking his head into the party and spoiling the fun.

JEFF. Shooting the polar bear.

ROSE. Yes, shooting the fucking polar bear. Pulling Sammy Spider's legs off.

JEFF. Milking Betty Moocow down to the gristle.

ROSE. Dropping Rita Pussycat down the well.

JEFF. Not a bad idea, to drown the whole smelly fantasy and get on with some constructive living.

ROSE. Constructive living. Oh yes, and how does one do that, being in love with a coward?

JEFF. Perhaps take some measure to cure the cowardice.

ROSE. Go boil you head in a bucket of–

JEFF. Really–That's the way out.

ROSE. What? A bucket of wee-wee?

JEFF. I can see the route broad and clear–*(Lights out.)*

ROSE. But why the hell should I?

JEFF. Something only you can do.

ROSE. When contact with you and your massive condradictions causes me nothing but pain?

JEFF. The love's not worth a light that doesn't hurt.

ROSE. Love, Jeff, love–ah, love–yes, love, old heavy purple summer love–Love hurts like music, sexual fatigue, like dying. Love hurts like dark eyes, searching kisses, hearts that heave and stir and stretch your muscles like a baby moving in your gut. Love hurts like thunderclouds and sunset gold and midnight dreams and old lost faces. Love does not hurt, not love, not my warm love, my love for you–It doesn't hurt like screaming snakes and broken glass and brain-damaged children. Not like war, Jeff. Love's not war.

JEFF. To the fucking death.

ROSE. No, no.

JEFF. To the death bed.

ROSE. Get away. No, don't come near me.

JEFF. To the last red gash.

ROSE. I love you. Piss off. Get out. I love you.

JEFF. Sing us a song then.
ROSE. I'll sing when I can fly.
JEFF. Fly by. Bird's thigh. *(Lights on.)*

ROSE *releases toy aeroplanes.* JEFF *shoots them down with pop gun.*

ROSE. Wart hog's wanky handy.
JEFF. Little cow's dairy bum.
ROSE. White rabbit's tit.
JEFF. Pussy cat's piss.
ROSE. Spider's turd.
JEFF. Camel sick.
ROSE. Monkey's wet diarrhoea.
JEFF. Fairy snot.
ROSE. Fairy snot.
JEFF. Fairy snot.
ROSE. Sing you a song now if you want.
JEFF. Not the one we used to sing at Weston-Super-Mare.
ROSE. It was a lovely little tune. Can you remember it?
JEFF *(at the piano.)* I think it went something like–
ROSE. That's the tune–sad little thing.
JEFF. Can you remember the words?
ROSE *(spoof Noel Coward tune).*

Don't cry
Gadfly.
Don't die
Meatpie.
Buy my potato stew.

Don't weep
Black sheep.
Don't sleep
Crawly creep.
I'm weeing over you.

First comes the dawn.
Then the frog spawn.
Lie on the lawn
With your frillies
All torn.

Don't sniff
Hippogriff.
Don't snort
Tiny wart.
I'm coming home to you.

ROSE. Birds build but not you.

Build nests I feather but not you.
Tweet, I tweet but hardly in public.
Mouse ears, how come, birds' wings. I soar on mouse wings.
You, great big elephant feet heavy limbs, no marrow, cover a fatty cushion. And that may help distribute the load evenly but hardly able to run and jump, let alone fly.
I soar. You great ugly thing. Large ears three feet by five feet (or one by one and a half millimetres.)
No ears I hear acute sound. No creeping up on me.
I peck, pecker up and fly with a herd of parrots, all colour, how splendid, oh no murky grey.
How sweet, dear things, and sing so nice. Oh no grear roar, but chirrup strain on the wind. How glad we are. Beady eye up in the trees, how watchful and hover swoop on the flea on my big friend.
And beaky dithery slithery wormy slimy down my throat with a strangulated cry.
And fruity screams and bees buzz. No good avoiding me.
I like eyes best, says the buzzard, best part. I like heart, says the falcon. I seed said the parrot as he flew into the elephant. Oh clumsy clod, you so high up invade my air space. I'll have to go higher.

JEFF. Oh nothing. I best little feathery thing. I lovely lumbering lollipop.

ROSE. Oh botty. I pretty polly with a truly delightful voice.

JEFF. But I a smashing clump of cuddles.

ROSE. But I a lithe lovely of ultimate grace.

JEFF. But I a great soft pile of pudding and taste truly delicious.

ROSE. You all too wet and sloppy. I lovely little lady all skippy and nice like fairy.

JEFF. No, you nasty like wiggly bogey. I definitely pleasant, all big bum and friendly farts.

ROSE. You smelly strong and make me faint. I gorgeous aroma of aphrodisiac.

JEFF. You arithritic aerial, crutchless and croaky. And I great nice household of hugs and kisses, and have very fine aristocratic nose.

ROSE. No, you colour only of spothead and blackie and very silly.

JEFF. I not silly.

Jack Show–The Rainbow Lady

Jack Show–The Rainbow Lady was performed in the Riley Smith Hall of Leeds University as part of the University Arts Festival of 1974.

Performers: Jeff Nuttall
Rose McGuire
Jim Duckett

Co-written with Rose McGuire

Enter JIM *and* JEFF*–comedians, long overcoats, trilby hats with the front brims turned up. Boogie round the hall, tripping up, waving etc.*

JEFF. I say, I say, I say.

JIM. What do you say you say you say?

JEFF. What colour, what colour is a sack of snot?

JIM. Oh dear, a sack of snot. What a thing to mention here in front of all these people. Would you like to borrow my–er–nankypuff?

JEFF. Well the nanky might do for a wank but you can go boil Your–

JIM. Balls to you ducky. I've got a question.

JEFF. You've got a question.

JIM. Specially for you. What is the shade of the drawers of a WRAAC sergeant?

JEFF. Shade, I think I'd rather get sunstroke. The shade of the nether undergarment of the Women's Royal Auxiliary Army Corps?

JIM. Never mind the auxiliaries. Get on with the sergeant.

JEFF. Fuck the sergeant. I'd rather fiddle with the privates.

JIM. Play with 'em all night night when you've answered my–

JEFF. The shade is–

JIM. Yes?

JEFF. The shade is–

JIM. Oh get on with it.

JEFF. How d'you make a Venetian blind?

JIM. I beg your pardon?

JEFF. Get him pissed.

JIM. Tombola in the gondola.

JEFF. Khaki.

JIM. What is?

JEFF. The shade of the military gusset.

JIM. Only at the closing of the day.

JEFF. You can't lick it.

JIM. Oh I don't know. . .

JEFF. Militant to the end. Head up. Tits out.

JIM. Head up? Smutty. Smutty. Green.

JEFF. What's green?

JIM. The colour I was referring to.

Spot on ROSE *in tower.*
Set–lighting tower rigged with five platforms. On all but the top platform are two chairs, One of each pair is red. The others are painted by ROSE *during the show. Top level is miscellaneous junk.*

Ist Level

ROSE *paints a green chair. On the ground floor* JIM *reads from his book about girls riding ponies.*

ROSE *(to the chair).* Oh don't you hobble home? How sick you look.
Let's hope a leg won't fall off.
And didn't you leave him so straight and tall?
A handsome young blade and such a compliment to me.

Ah how the tall do totter. Crisis in the Crimea. Balaclava did you badly with no Lady of the Lamp to help you out.
How I hope your back stays straight.
For you a corner where you won't clash.
This is my gangly gangrene friend.

JEFF *and* JIM *introduce one another in a song–classic vaudeville routine– Oh Mr Nuttall, Oh Mr Ducket. Sick lyrics.*

ROSE. We used to like to walk for miles.
We used to make a bed of spring corn.
We used to watch water weeds tangle in flashes of sunlight.
We used to climb great hills till they didn't seem so steep and tree trunks began to slide to babyshit. Our own private First World War.
Till we changed our trenches for concrete. A wise move I thought.
Till you came home, your hard crust only mouldy over pulp. For you a place of uneasy combinations,
My gangrene friend.
JIM. I say, I say, I say.
JEFF *(different tone).* I say! I say! I say!
JIM. What colour is a Glasgow Ranger?
JEFF. You mean a Texas longhorn?
JIM. The team that plays Celtic.
JEFF. You mean a rough Girl Guide?
JIM. Why are you obsessed with little girls?
JEFF. Why? Have you got something else to recommend?
JIM. I wouldn't share anything with you.
JEFF. Oh come on Jim, don't sulk.
JIM. I'm not feeling very merry.
JEFF. A little bit blue?

JIM *sings blue song.* JEFF *at piano.*

2nd Level

ROSE *paints a blue chair.* JIM *and* JEFF *go into circus routine with* JIM *as the performing animal.* ROSE *mimics* JEFF *using the chair as performer.*

JIM. Now I want to be a lion.
JEFF. No you can be seal.
JIM. Lion.
JEFF. Seal.
JIM. Lion.
JEFF. Seal.
JIM. You can be a seal.
JEFF. I'm ring-master.
JIM. You'll never master my ringpiece, that's for sure.
JEFF. I'm the guy with big black whip.
JIM. I'll be seal.
JEFF. Right, what I want you to do is stand on your head on the lady over there.

Improvisation.

JEFF. For your next trick, Sandra Seal, I want you to eat this fish. *(Flashes.)*

Improvise.

JEFF. And finally I want you to tell me what is long and thin and makes a van cough.
JIM. A Chevrolet choke?
JEFF. A Bedford belch.
JIM. A Vaulkswagon vomit?
JEFF. A sunflower.
JIM *(Soppy).* Ah-h-h-h. . .
JEFF. What is it that's yellow and sloppy that you sniff at the bottom of the garden?
JIM. A sunflower.
JEFF. No. A bucket of shit.
JIM. What a nasty fellow.
JEFF. Well, nearly yellow. . .

3rd Level

ROSE *paints chair yellow. During her speech* JEFF *and* JIM *do a 'Roland and Shirley'–i.e. spoof of Miller-Cameron.*

ROSE.
Whiter than white in black and white.
A clean advertisement.
Let's have no more argument. Traditional black taffeta is not the colour for shrouds.
Yes, I know it's normal. Those big full skirts, the blouse carefully done up with covered buttons. Covered in black taffeta.
Yes, it's shiny but not right for a shroud.
African brown which isn't brown at all but light mottled beige.

Yes a bit hippy. But what whiter than white in this black and white.
How dull is real white. No mother, you have not done well today.
But see how bright a white is this.
How clean. But how unkeen the eyesight was.
Now we can tell. Look at the corpse, how thick the lens, how big the eyes look now, two years, eight, nine? Why whisper two when I can see the great magnifying glasses?
And why laid out now two years, eight, nine, in black taffeta?
African brown which is beige and nine years is the right time.
Let's do the whole thing properly.
And change the colour to make it brighter than white on black and white in the flicker of a soap packet.

JIM. I say, I say, I say.
JEFF. I say, I say, I say.
JIM. What's pimply and contributes to South African aid?
JEFF. Douglas-Home.
JIM. No you twit. An orange.
JEFF. Edward Heath.
JIM. An orange, dope.
JEFF. Porridge and soap? Don't be carbolic.
JIM. Oh scrub off.

4th Level

ROSE *very meticulously paints a chair orange.* JEFF *and* JIM *do imitation of* ROSE– 'Guess who this is. Who said this?' *etc.*

ROSE.
Aren't you bright?
Tangerine gash, a merry fruit.
One last piece of corny symbolism and let's see where we are.
Not the highest level. My sparkly friend is not as bright as me.
Bright as an abortion and happy as a holocaust. Me, I shall go higher.
See if you can deepen. A little too frivolous as yet, and that shows a superficial intellect, a passionate nature not in line with profundity.
Though here is not the place to indulge in antique verbiage.
We require comprehension.
When the weather changes we go out to play.
When the sky darkens we stay in and play dirty lexicon, and a great deal, change flash to slash and shit to shat.
When it snows see what pretty paint is on our faces, and we buy warm boots. We are snug.
But I'm much snugger than you. How well I shine.

JEFF. I think she wants to speak to us.
JIM. Who?

JEFF. The princess in the fuckin' tower.
JIM. Fuckin' tower?
JEFF. Do what you like with it.
JIM. What does she wish to impart?

ROSE *hurls object.*

JEFF. I think she wants to attract our attention.
JIM. I think she's inviting us up for a–
JEFF. A jump?
JIM. I was going to say a cup of tea.

ROSE *hurls cup of tea.*

ROSE. Put it on.
JIM. Oh listen. She's not taking any risks.
ROSE. Dress up in it.
JEFF. One of those weirdos.

5th Level

ROSE *passes down the junk to* JIM *and* JEFF *on ropes,* JIM *and* JEFF *dress up in it.*

JIM *sings his song.*

Add action for JIM *and* JEFF *while* ROSE *is painting chairs.*

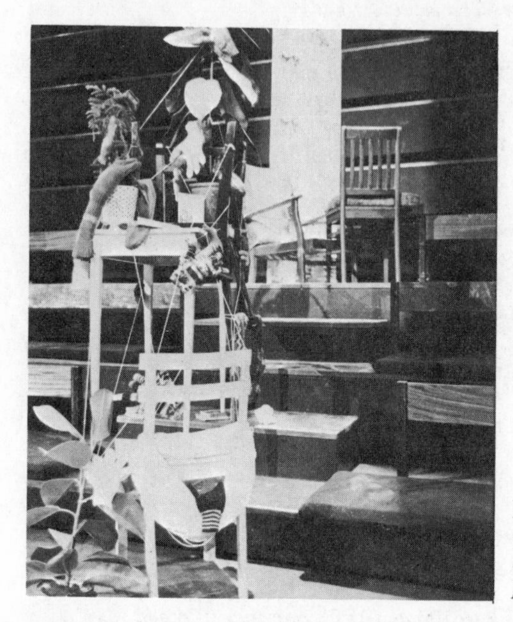

Rose's Greetings Cards show at the Cockpit—1974.
Photo: José Nava

'Jack' at the Cockpit The author reads a greetings card, Rose addressed herself to the hanging heads (with kettles).
Photo: José Nava

The author talks to the kettles. Cockpit Theatre–1974
Photo: José Nava

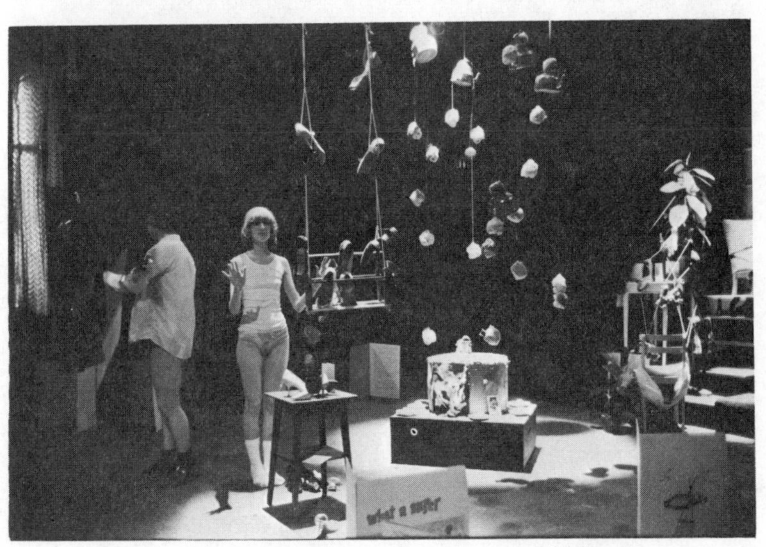

Rose with shoes, Cockpit Theatre–1974
Photo: José Nava

Jack Show–A Sip at the Beepot

Jack Show–A Sip at the Beepot was performed at the Oval Theatre, early 1974.

Performers: Jeff Nuttall
Rose McGuire
Lol Coxhill

Co-written with Rose McGuire

Presentation One

JEFF. With the Andamanese we have the unique opportunity of observing what the untutored human being is like—an adult creature possessed of the intellectual capacity of a child of ten or twelve when bred in civilisation. He has a very short though strong memory. He is vain and, while under the spur of vanity, industrious and persevering. He is suspicious of, but hospitable to, strangers. He is teachable up to a quickly reached limit, fond of undefined games and practical jokes. I am Walter Pigeon, seasoned lawyer. Shy. Stand in front, adjust my flies. Hide my hands.

JEFF *moves into a net, in a cage.*

ROSE. Now I have you in a nutshell, in a conch shell, in a fingernail. Now I have you encased in a musselshell, a snail's house, a toenail. Muscle Beach is as good a place to fish for fellows as anywhere. Up comes the net and look what I've got!

JEFF. When an evil spirit has been caught by the doctor priest of the village it is put into a small ornamented scape boat, built for the purpose and towed out to sea. Should the boat land at another village and transfer the spirit there an attack with quarter staves under recognised rules is made on the makers of the boat. I am Gary Cooper whooping it up on Main Street surrounded by dead spoils. Let me surrender in your arms, foil the gaze of the fans.

ROSE. Now I have you as a trophy, a specimen, a piece of evidence from beyond the shores of Chinese Guatemala. A hippogryph, a catawomb, a catalyst, a eucalep. One legged, one eyed cyclopod, a sciopod, a boot that bounds across the farthest Steppes, the Town Hall steps, the back door steps, the cathedral steps of darkest Africa.

JEFF. When relatives meet after a long absence they sit huddled together in groups, weeping and howling in each others' arms. There is no such difference observable between the signs of joy and grief on such occasions. Montgomery Clift cleft on the palate of Nevada. Let me hide my eyes. A man can't cry.

ROSE. I present the Philliponian sponge fish scooped from the warm womb waters of the Mountbatten Islands, bottled for the homeward voyage in a tub of rum, renowned in the courts of eighteenth century Spain as an instrument of song. When prodded makes a fluting noise to well surprise the shrieks of the Philliponian Philharmonic.

JEFF. After a fight between two villages there is a peace-making ceremony. The men of the village who made the attack erect a screen against which they stand, while the women beat time with their hands on their thighs. The men of the other party then dance in front of them. Each dancer seizes one of the standing men by the shoulders and leaps up and down before him giving him a good shaking. After the dance both parties weep together and exchange weapons. He is Clark Gable fond. Let me lie back and be the lady.

ROSE. I present the Appalachian Brontophile. Found in a state of incipient drool at the Gate of Paradise (a holiday motel of most extraordinary propensities) the Bront, as he was fondly dubbed by Jane Fonda, humps and grunts and smirks and smiles at all the candidates who wish to pass their honeymoons as angels of the honeycraters. Never allowed to sip at the beepot the unfortunate and ill-aspected Bront expells his grief in whiffs and sniffles for everybody's edification.

Presentation Two

JEFF.

Now I want to go to sea. In a schooner, glass of Lager, on the prairie, land sea, of sea wheat–tastes fishy.
Now I want to unravel wastes. How vast!
Now I see the generalities. Take a note, no particulars. I care little, smell the breeze.
Silly man, I see the sea–salty rolls, dry desert, salt lake, damp mormon. What power over the ladies and get in a glue. How sticky gum on my feet.
Oh see, my wheels all stuck. Bogged down. Fen around, rising.

Oh mother, I'm coming home but only to get clean.

JEFF *climbs into little trolley with sail.*

ROSE. Now I've cast you adrift in a sticky sea. Now I've shoved you up shit creek without a paddle. Now my wishes can direct you to the Amazon, the Upper Thames, the Straits of Oxbridge, the Azores, the Monkey's Paws, the Baboon's Bum, or the Running Sores of the Antipodes.

JEFF. Oh brave I travel, waggle rudder, trundle on the Old-Hio. High it carries me, my little sail, sturdy through the seamier sides of life and steaming waddies (and that, by the way, means waterholes).
Oh mother, here I come. I've eaten my fairy cakes, so fill my case with bath buns.

ROSE. Ladies and gentlemen, I present the hobble-crate. This is the charioteer that circled the sphere at Brand's Hatch in the space of a conker match.

JEFF. Here's not to overestimate my exploits. The nasty poison darts that bite my knackers. The naked fly that likes my sweat.

The gorgeous orchid sees my blood and turns my hair quite grey.
Much more in kindness than subversion did I soothe the anaconda.
Not out of fear do caymans croon to my unholy growth.
Of comfort there is little, but oh Mother, the fever has got me. I'm coming home but only for a laxative.

ROSE. With axles aspin and a flick knife on either hub he carved through the Nazi hordes on a dull day at Porthcawl, leaving behind him a mess of wretches loosed from their moorings, their limbs unsocketed, noses askew, eyeballs extended to heaven beseeching a wind or raincloud.
Alone, with nothing to assist him but an outboard motor this redoubtable land-yachtsman circled the Scilly Isles seven times rumbling over the rocks and skimming the beaches. The leeches that clung to his scrotum did nothing to stop him, apart from eroding the rope of his scrotum, thus tapping his emergency power resources.

JEFF. Mother, I'm coming home but only for apple pie, the pig stye and an extra helping of big feather bed. Now no more to stroll the jungle, trample the mango, strum the banjo. All I want is a home in the haven, heaven of mutton and a sewn-on shirt button. Gone are the jaguars and panthers and piranhas. Mum I'm coming home but only to refuel.

ROSE. The forces that drive the spheres blow out his belly, conducting him splendidly over the pastures of purgatory. The farts of the graces propel him amazingly, driving the vehicle faster than bicycles, rain cycles, spectacles of moon rockets.

JEFF. Give me my anorak mum.

ROSE. Where will he land, this flying Englishman?

JEFF. Kill me dad, mum.

ROSE. Far from the splash of Trafalgar Square pigeons.

JEFF. Too much water in me orange-juice mum.

ROSE. Far from the cries of the neglected wives.

JEFF. The albatross is a terrible bird, mum.

ROSE. Down on the ocean bed at the brink of the fish quarries.

Presentation Three

JEFF. Let me be your birthday present
Let me be your own true card
Let me send you love and kisses
Mr Postman don't be hard.

Let me be your Christmas present
Wrap me up all nice and bright
Postman dump me on her doorstep
In the early morning light.

Tie me up with string and Sellotape
Hide my face with postage stamps
Pop me in your woolly stocking
Light the Christmas fairy lamps.

I'm a bunch of big red roses
I'm a cuddly teddy bear
I'm a box that's all soft centres
You're the one for whom I care.

JEFF *is tied up in a mad parcel with lot of silly things stuck in the string.*

ROSE. I see you in your long divisions. Now I can grasp your multiplications, subtract your inadequacies, add your seasoning. Now I can deal with your splits down the middle.

JEFF. I bring you your eighteenth birthday cake and I'll thank the neighbours not to laugh. Shaped like a top hat and nicely covered in sugar jellies, an odd Smarty thrown in. I bring you a cake shaped like a top hat inside also, filled with synthetic cream and real strawberries. Sometimes nature approaches art, and I'll thank you to eat it all.

ROSE. How do you form a perspective on prisms? What is the correct way to address a man of deliberate schizoid character forms? Do you stand to the left or the right? Front or back? Up or down? Or do you stand in the middle like a traffic warden trying to sort out the streams, to direct all characteristics of the same weight, colour and speed into more or less the same direction? Not that I'm trying to direct anything here, oh no, I wouldn't dare. This character's already built a house in his head with a dozen rooms, walls three foot thick, soundproof, and no doors.

JEFF. I bring you two long-playing records. On the one hand the Mills Brothers, a paper moon and a paper doll are ashes to the glow-worm on a sluggish river. On the other hand the Foxes, Charlie and Inez, are all over-heart-rending Via Con Dios and dammit, I've been posted again.

ROSE. He thinks I live in one of them. He has my room arranged with lascivious silks and underwear, flock walls and fountains, Babycham and maiden's water, a palace of fetishes halfway between Sarah Bernhardt's boudoir and an Army Married Quarters warehouse. Here, he informs me, his true self reclines, assuming that the passivity that comes with complete relaxation in some way guarantees authenticity. 'You and just you know the real me,' he says. 'I'm all for you, completely yours when the *truth* is told.'

JEFF. I bring you see-through knickers, saggy Y-fronts, if you let me watch you wee. I bring you Thames and Hudson if you let me read your mind.

ROSE. In another room is a field of daisies where he shows his mother his newly brushed locks, his head bowed in prayer. God himself dwells in this chamber with a benificence strong enough to reduce the Vietnam holocaust, the weaknesses of bad men and the face of Richard Nixon to an abstract zero, a beaming, chuckling god leaning out of the sun's rondel and singing like a fucking cuckoo clock.

JEFF. I bring you the dream of Adam and Eve. I use my rib as a scalpel. I cut away one growth covered in hairs and teeth, one ovary, one fallopian tube and one appendix. I present them to you in ancient mythology. I use my rib as a needle to sew you up, to tie you up. I give you an image of imagined death to split the stitches.

ROSE. Yet another chamber holds a hatchet-faced gangster aged fifteen, mouthful of Bogart, eyes full of Buchenwald newsreels, phrases like 'old before his time' and 'eyes that have seen too much too soon' running down the slanted Woodbine out of his narcissistic skull.

JEFF. I bring you the picture of a slaughtered childhood in a slop bucket under the sink. I give you an outsize maternity sanitary towel to make the blood less human.

ROSE. In another room, a very public room with glass walls a jellied amoeba with no will or speech plays with an extension of his eggslime body that promises, with continuous whimpering encouragement, to become a penis.

JEFF. But most of all, at the end of the ball, after the last waltz, after your solitary mental meanderings, after your trivial obsessions and after the curtains are drawn, I bring you a lump that may be fat, I bring you a body that might be slack, I bring you a heart that might be weak, but at least I bring you me.

ROSE. Further chambers hold mirrors wherein to escape, ambitions whereon to ride, and a final chamber stacked with plum pies, jam butties, fish and chips, and pints and pints and pints (and pints and pints and pints and pints) of Tetley's bitter.

Presentation Four

JEFF.

Now I shall be a handsome devil.
Now you'll see me in a true light.
Now you can see how the angle of my nose indicates a noble nature.
Now you perceive I'm slim and lithe, graceful and agile, brave and hardy, annual, perennial, bilingual and singularly fine.
Invent a good story for this one. I feel great stirrings within me.

JEFF *moves onto pedestal, military jacket, mutters compliments to himself throughout.*

ROSE. Now I have you, your feet an inch from my adoring lip. Now I have you raised aloft where you can shit voluminously upon my Drene shampoo. Now I have you rigged up on a system of pulleys so you can glower at me through a gap in the clouds.

JEFF. Sometimes I'm a warrior, sometimes I'm a lover, and sometimes I'm a sad little in-between.

ROSE. Ladies and gentlemen, I give you the Leader, the Father, the biggest prick of all time.
I give you the tall tit perched on the podium, the fetish god of City Square, the long dark shadow that stands in the bedroom door and says 'Time little girls were asleep.'
I give you the general, the equestrian statue, the only support for a plumed helmet, the sabre wagger, standard bearer, fabled vertical that stalks out of Wellington in jackboots, on to Churchill with his wings up, on to Stalin with his sickle hammered hot, back to Hitler with his Reichstag going up in smoke.
I give you the power and the glory, A-fucking-men, the Nation's proud story, the pomp that was Rome, the head of the home, the mountainous moustache, the arrogant eyelash, the puffed out thorax, the indubitable fact, the first and last, Uncle Jack's axe, our glorious past.
I give you Caesar seizing a grip on the weaklings.
I give you Napoleon nibbling the nipples of Josephine.
Alexander the Great grating the faces of Africa down to the bone.
Al Capone pondering.
Mussolini muscle-building.
Neitzsche preaching.
Beethoven's oven.
Kierkegaard's garden.
Big Daddy with his boots and spurs on.
Yahweh, Jove, Jehova, Zeus, God the Patterfam, smack yer arse, stick his baton in yer gob and fuck yer stupid.

Presentation Five

JEFF. BlackJack Ketchem on the gallows, badly tied noose. Release the trapdoor. Black Kack's head wrenched from his shoulders, the quick cry completely unrelated to the final ejaculation. Who wrenches his prick from his knackers? Who can sort out desire from an erection? Bury my wish away from my action. A tomb for my head, a grave for the land mass.

JEFF *moves into box with his head sticking out.*

ROSE. Now I've done it. Off at the neck. Reduced you to intellect. . . No more ache of frustration lighting up the crutch like Verey lights. Only toothache, earache, neuralgia and angst.

JEFF. Who knows what there is in my box?
How many moles and how many mushrooms, how many grapes and how many raisins, in how many clusters or how many bunches?
How many packages and cartons and bottles could you get into this box?
How fly, tart, sharp or fruity are my digestive juices?
How acute is my intake beyond the point of absolute secrecy, utter solemnity, perfect sincerity, hopeless inaccuracy?

ROSE. Ladies and gentlemen, this is the oracle. This is the orifice mouthing the future. Look, look into those misty eyes. Look at the distant skies, far blue beyond, the seagulls' despond.

JEFF. Syntactical eptopic TV, hydraulic hyperbolic hiatus.
Kidney machination, iron lung and head hung, make me the man of the future.
Forgotten yearnings, no prick, no past.
The vast computer, store-house of knowledge, telepathic tell-tale-tit. It will all be explained scientifically eventually.

ROSE. Touch it if you can, ladies and gents, the wisdom in those even teeth. The careful tongue that lies beneath.

JEFF. Evacuate ejaculation, filch my flatulence. No shit, no shellshock, no adrenalin, no amnesia.

ROSE. Read the directions on his even breath. See beyond the shores of death. See beyond the mountain peak. See and find the cause to seek.
You want to know the height of the Andes? Ask him.

JEFF. 278 times 83 equals 47032 backwards.

ROSE. You want to know the angle of the dangle of Marlon Brando? Pop your question.

JEFF. The bat is the only animal other than a primate that has a free penis.

ROSE. You want to demand the secrets bubbling in the back skulls of the great political leaders? No problem.

JEFF. A Masai warrior sleeps on his left side with his head resting on his left arm. His arm is crooked and positioned so as to avoid the ear. In this way the warrior may still be able to pick up vibrations from the ground. His right leg is straight. His left leg is bent at the knee, the left heel touching the right knee. In this way the left thigh provides a comfortable rest for the Masai warrior's genitals.

ROSE. You want to quell your fear, stop your anxiety, sleep well at night? Climb to the height of the achievement? Get rid of your sense of bereavement? Step this way.

JEFF. The heat five feet under the surface of the earth is sufficient to boil five gallons of water an hour.

ROSE. This man knows the width of the Bridge of Sighs, the way up Raquel Welch's thighs, the depth of the wails of the bad souls, how to get over the Styx and set up a Butlin's.

JEFF. The question as to whether the helical fossil, the devil's corkscrew, which can be left or right-handed, is the fossil of a long-extinct twining plant, or the cast of a helical burrow made by the ancestor of the modern beaver, was settled when the remains of small beavers were found in some of them.

ROSE. How to conduct a Shibboleth in your own garden.

JEFF. The instruments used for pedicure should not be used for manicure.

ROSE. Where to hear the mouthing vagina of the Whore of Babylon.

JEFF. By 1853 a thousand ships were arriving in Melbourne every day.

ROSE. Where to store your seed at a midnight manipulation.

JEFF. The Burke expedition set out to explore the Australian interior on August the 9th, 1860.

ROSE. How to address a letter to the Ministry of Smoky Jokes.

JEFF. The disappearance of the plague from Europe in the 17th and 18th Centuries coincided with the appearance of the brown sewer rat.

ROSE. Where to locate the mate of the Lugger now that the Marie Celeste has run aground.

JEFF. The advent of the motor-car has occasioned an evolutionary change in the common hedgehog. It no longer curls up into a ball at the first sign of danger. It runs.

ROSE.
What to say in an emergency.
What to do in a quandary.
What to sell in an infirmary.
How to save the day, get to Blackpool, start up the old bus, mend the puncture in the back tyre, wire up a dummy for sound and procure an erection from a week-old corpse.
The truth, ladies and gentlemen, lies here.

Audience invited to ask question of the oracle. JEFF'*s answers should be more pieces of useless information, whatever the question.*

Presentation Six

JEFF.
Make me a slimy snake, slippery eel.
Make me a single shape, flexible tube all slither to whispering rustle through silk, to slow worm, to all apertures. The lovely young parasite.
Grease me green, verdant of Eden, original colour, camouflage from God, sneaky fucker, hiding in ferns to wait for the big mistake.
Make me long and round and smooth out the lumps, no limbs to hinder the passage. Carry to darkest places, the softest purple of sun sets in your wet, wet cunt.
Cream my skin to startle a silver snail's trail across the bone shadow thrown from your body.
First mark. Original sin, Stream of vomit is the dawn light of history.

JEFF *is naked.* ROSE *wraps him in plastic and covers him with vaseline.* JEFF *wears a bathing cap.*

ROSE. Now I've got you in the palm of my hand like a broken yolk. Now I've got you running down my leg in a cold wind as I make my way to the bus-stop. Now I've got you under my tongue, rattling in my throat, collecting in a dense sheen at my gusset.
JEFF. Make me a gob of frog-spawn to run luxurious on a cat's thigh.
ROSE. This I promise you all, is the origin of the species. This little mountain of mucoid substance is the ocean floor that spawned a million molluscs. If you place your ear to the mouth of a mole-hole you can hear a music akin to that of the spheres a music that passes like voices of coupling dead, rises like odours and honeydew, swift from the tip of this curious biological phenomenon.
JEFF. Make me a backbone like the belly of a pig to sweeten the salt water.

ROSE *fondles prick, music swells, an overlay of wind in telephone wires, reed pipes and delicate voices.*

ROSE.
This, ladies and gentlemen, is the earliest form of life.
When the water was divided from the dry land,
When the first light shimmered dimly at the edge of the mud flats this singing little person dragged his cells together and proceeded to gestate.
Somewhere in the midst of this translucent substance a nucleus cuddles. Always the black spot is the frogspawn centre. Somewhere in this boneless head an idea is toying with its tenderest possibilities that will flower in a billion years into a statement like 'Eureka' or 'You stink' or 'I feel like a spot of hanky panky'.

Somewhere in this watery flab is the substance destined to be bone and the song of the spheres that it sings just now will become a moan, a cry indicating that life has recognised itself rather than merely playing with its–er–vulnerabilities. Hark, hark. Is that the first declaration of existence?

JEFF. I am. I am. I am about to ejaculate.

He does so if possible.

Jack Show–The Saga of San Foo and the Black Watch Beetle

Jack Show—The Saga of San Foo and the Black Watch Beetle was performed on tour late 1973, early 1974.

Performers: Jeff Nuttall
Rose McGuire

Co-written with Rose McGuire

Five minutes of ROSE *walking. Nostalgic French music.* JEFF *knocking.* ROSE *makes a room in one corner of the area during her speech.*

ROSE. Holy Mary, mother of pigs
Go into the man's heart and heal it.
Holy Mary, dug where beggars feed
Lead him beyond me to browse on his idiot buttercups.
Holy Mary get the wet bastard off my doorstep with his
whimpering and his jelly flesh.
Holy Mary lovesick beast croon in his waxy ear and get him
off my back.
Knocking.
Let him recover from his unfortunate wounds.
Go lick out his ulcers for me.
Leave me a cooling triviality.
My toys and my pleasure.
Leave me alone to have a drink for Christ's sake.
Knocking.
He can dither all night. It doesn't hurt me.
Oh dear me look what God's dumped on the doorstep.
A little dollop of angel shit anxious to be loved for its
noble aspirations.
Knocking.
Oh dear me, look what the cat's brought up,
One of those ropes of half-digested rat hair, one of those
choice little offerings.
Knocking.
It gets in my head and gives me a headache.
It gets in my plans and throws them wrong.
Knocking, knocking, thumping, drumming.
Well, what do you want?
Have you come for another nuzzle at my thighs?
Are you going to have another crack at making me into your
mother?

JEFF *enters, very dignified. Moves the room to another corner very carefully.*

JEFF. And the cupboard was bare.
ROSE. In the chest of drawers.
JEFF. Where's the whiskey?
ROSE. I'll get it.
JEFF. No, just tell me where it is.
ROSE. I'll get it I said.

JEFF. Where's the saucy cup?
ROSE. In the filing cabinet.
JEFF. Who's the roundelay?
ROSE. In the pink.
JEFF. Is it in the other room?
ROSE. Can't you get anything into your thick bonce?
JEFF. The kitchen then?
ROSE. Out to play, lost in the garden.
JEFF. In the lounge, idly loafing?
ROSE. Shut up.
JEFF. In the window glinting in the sunlight?
ROSE. I'll get the bloody whiskey.
JEFF. Under the bed in a puff of dust?
ROSE. I'll get the bloody fucking whiskey.
JEFF. Oh don't bother.
ROSE. What?
JEFF. Don't feel like a drink really.
ROSE. Kiss me.

ROSE *leaves.* JEFF *puts on a romantic orchestral record and tells the story, improvised, of the mystic San Foo and the Black Watch Beetle.*

ROSE *(off).* I'll be ready in a minute.
JEFF. You're hypnotised by your own mediocre looks.
ROSE. What?
JEFF. I said you're a vain bitch.
ROSE. Just doing my eyes.
JEFF. I'm coming in.
ROSE. I'll be out in a minute. Stay where you are.
JEFF. I'll come and zip you up.
ROSE. I'm zipped up.
JEFF. I'll strip you off then.
ROSE. I'll be in in a minute.
JEFF. There's no bed in there.
ROSE. Don't take me for granted.
JEFF. I'll take you for nothing.
ROSE. Stay where you are.

JEFF *moves towards door.* ROSE *comes in pale and ragged smeared with blood and filth, bright new ribbons in her hair. She rearranges the room and hooks herself into place in it. She starts building her Green Friend–a little man made of vegetables.*

JEFF. You're the cream of the crop
ROSE. Lardy di da.
JEFF. You're the tip of the iceberg.
ROSE. Doody di doo.
JEFF. You're the highest mountain.
ROSE. Hi ho.
JEFF. You're the deepest ocean.

ROSE. Hoo ha.
JEFF. You're the Colosseum!
ROSE. Slimy snail, stray cat catching the purple rat in a lightning flash on a very dark wet night.
Pretty bee, you can't catch me. I'm much too sharp.
JEFF. Yum yum.
ROSE. I drink the three spurts at the fountain and even if I don't see Jesus I know I've got my protein.
I'm a lovely joint at a time of inflation. An indulgent pursuit in a dim crisis. I take my pleasure seriously. I can tell when someone's lying.
JEFF. You angelic dip of nectar.
ROSE. Has he told you the story of silly San Foo
Who followed a beetle up Mount Smelly Poo?
Well he made it up. It isn't true.

During the following dialogue ROSE *makes silly noises on the swanee whistle.* JEFF *plays sloppy songs on a toy grand piano.*

JEFF. I've never seen anything as beautiful as you.
ROSE. You've never seen beauty.
JEFF. I must be with you all the time. I must touch you.
ROSE. I must escape forever. I must crush you.
JEFF. You only say vicious things to illuminate my adoration.
ROSE. I say vicious things to foul you, to destroy you.
JEFF. You can't foul me. I love too well.
ROSE. Nobody loves too well for death.
JEFF. What is death?
ROSE. Shit.
JEFF. Where is death?
ROSE. Up your arse.

ROSE *silently superintends the moving of the room to the original corner.* JEFF *does the carrying.*

ROSE.
Did he tell you how the visionary San Foo had a hiatus hernia.
Did he tell you how the visionary San Foo wore a woolly in bed to soak up the perspiration?
Did he tell you how the little beetle put talcum powder at the bottom of the bed where the visionary San Foo's feet lay?
Did he tell how the visionary San Foo was only a second candidate for Nirvana because he couldn't always control his bowels on the way to the pub?
Well that's true.
JEFF. Where do dreams come from Rose?
ROSE. Bone and flesh and wood and sap.
JEFF. Love, the spirit and the visiting grace. What do you dream with Rose?
ROSE. Messy labia and gungy grey matter. The wood man and the

snake man and the sea outside my window. Cup cake and cream caramels. Go away. I want to play.

JEFF. Frolic in the pigsty sporting with the porkers?

ROSE. Not last night I didn't.

JEFF. Hanging upside down, growing green algae and whispering 'Pity me?'

ROSE. Not for two days.

JEFF. You smell worse than a fish and chip shop.

ROSE. I'm a zoo keeper, keeping animal muscle for ever and ever until the end.

JEFF. We won't fry up completely, Rose. Were you snappy last night?

ROSE. I tended extremities.

JEFF. Were you deliciously relaxed last night Rose?

ROSE. Slowing down as time goes on. Not much longer now, but not last night.

JEFF. What were you doing last night?

ROSE. I was–in my room.

JEFF. Who were you with in your room?

ROSE. God and his dirty angels.

JEFF. You know no Gods. You know no eternity. You're the most mortal creature living.

ROSE. Living?

JEFF. With soiled cherubim it seems.

ROSE. Mortality is the only way to know death.

JEFF. And what fouls the angels?

ROSE. Me with my decay.

JEFF. Get stuffed.

ROSE. You can't make a monument out of me.

JEFF. I'll build you a garden in the sky.

ROSE. That'll take a lot of money.

JEFF. No, just takes faith and dreams.

ROSE. Oh, beg your pardon. I thought you meant a real garden.

ROSE *ties* JEFF *up in a bundle.*

ROSE, Shall I make a gesture towards you?
Shall I give you a push along the way?
Go over to your side, help to further your very deep desires?
Creep like a toadstool over your body? Holy fungus.
First the extremities, then the limbs. I can't help the features.
They'll stay for a while.
Bye bye bits of body.
No more nasty pimples, but ugly blotches, or perhaps your
skin will turn delicate translucent. How lovely, how transcendent.
An ethereal disease.
He based his story on Robert the Bruce who was a leper.

While JEFF *sings* ROSE *arranges another room with 'precious objects' and the best parts of the other room.*

JEFF. Why do you use me?
Why now reduce me?
I'm not a piece of wood.
I'm not a tool
Though I may be a fool
To imagine our love could be good.

Why don't you spoil me
Completely destroy me?
I can't last much longer now.
Why don't you spill me?
You might as well kill me.
I know you're the wrong girl now.

We could have climbed a mountain.
We could have reached the peak.
We could have sailed the ocean
Before we sprung a leak.

Go where the cash is.
Scatter my ashes.
I'll be glad to blow away.
Or cut all my limbs loose,
Drown me with love juice.
Tomorrow's another day.

ROSE. It doesn't look pretty,
Your snot on my titty
So don't weep all over me now.
Oh please spare my poor heart.
The fumes of a wet fart.
You can't come to tea with me now.

It doesn't look happy
Your teeth black and gappy.
Don't kiss my rectum yet.
Your armpits are sweaty
Like my cousin Betty.
Some guys are dry, some wet.

I could have thrown you over.
I could have lived my life.
We could have gone to Dover.
You could have left your wife.

It's overdue now.
Pig's poo to you now.
You can go boil your head.
I'll wash the sheet.
No more smelly old feet.
The next one won't soil the bed.

ROSE *cuts off* JEFF's *wrappings, takes them to her new room, makes a bed out of them and gets under it, with toys and 'precious objects'.*

ROSE *talks to herself while emptying suitcase of nasty things.* JEFF *calls* 'Rose, Rose. . .'

JEFF. Rose.
ROSE. Oh don't.
JEFF. Go swing on a grating and drop down a drain.
ROSE. How unpleasant.
JEFF. Rose.
ROSE. Oh well, I suppose so.
JEFF. Go vomit up wallpaper patterns at Harrods.
ROSE. How curious.
JEFF. Rose.
ROSE. Oh good.
JEFF. Go steal a bus, and buzz off to Brighton.
ROSE. How recreational.
JEFF. Rose.
ROSE. Oh what now?
JEFF. Go balance on one tit down by the river.
ROSE. Oh chill.
JEFF. Rose.
ROSE. Shut your face.
JEFF. Go gobble wogs, fuck tinkers, suck sugar cubes.
ROSE. Stay out of the bedroom.

ROSE *gets out of bed and barricades the room using four chairs as posts at corners of the room, maybe, with string wound round them like a fence.*

ROSE. Speech to be written when Rose is inspired.
JEFF. Let's all wait for Rose's inspiration.
Let's all wait while Rose's fingers have another dig at her less than mortal, let's say mundane, body.
Rose is having another wank.
Rose is have another scratch at her twat.
Rose is playing another game of patience.
Rose is building another mouldy structure.
Rose is not waiting for a visitation or even a visit, just avoiding the possibility.
And if my body doesn't work very well, I'm not an object of fun.
And leprosy isn't a disease or an example of human endeavour, it's more a noble aspiration.
So what if I am subject to pain in the middle of the night?
What if my bum is a bit dicey? I'd say that made me more worthy.
I went in the bedroom last night.
ROSE. Oh yes.
JEFF. I saw everything.
ROSE. Oh did you.

ROSE. Good good.
JEFF. I saw the pubic hair on the pillow.
ROSE. How minute.
JEFF. I saw the--
ROSE. Yes what?
JEFF What do you think I saw?
ROSE. I don't know. No idea. What do you think you saw?
JEFF. You know what I saw.
ROSE. You saw nothing. You haven't been in my bedroom.
JEFF. I will one day.
ROSE. You stay here. Live your life. Don't give yourself any nasty shocks.

Jack Show–Sunday Blood

Jack Show–Sunday Blood was performed throughout the summer and autumn of 1974 at the Oval Theatre, the Edinburgh Festival Poetry Session at the Adam House Theatre, the Coelfrith Arts Centre, Sunderland as part of the Writers Forum Week End, at the Swarthmore Arts Centre, Leeds.

Performers: Jeff Nuttall
Rose McGuire

Co-scripted with Rose McGuire

Live music by Lol Coxhill

Two platforms at opposite ends of the space, festooned with hanging geometric shapes cut out in hardboard and painted in primary colours. Each platform is fitted with a buzzer to be operated by the foot. Other sundry objects used in the action are hanging among the suspended shapes. Enter ROSE *and* JEFF *amongst the audience, off the platforms.*

ROSE. First there was Thomas and Florence, Tom and Flo, Sparr Sparrowlegs and Large and Handsome, Mad and Clever. Poor Tommy, little fellow. Lived twelve years in Shrewsbury Hospital.

JEFF. Call a parliamentary investigation and let him be the first out.

ROSE. Shell shocked tumble down the roof to worry where are my lost children. I am not a tangled mass of blood and brains.

JEFF. All he got was a broken collar bone and a stretch in just about the worst place you could go. What a name it had then!

ROSE. Twelve years living unmeant death. Not terrifying, like Dracula—the Mother Superior planning the conversion of 2000 nuns.

JEFF. All we need is a down payment.

ROSE. Not mad. I sit and dream. Do I tell my dreams? Who to? I mutter. Hands convulsively snatch my flies. More children yet to father. Florence, my 1890's mound of flesh.

JEFF. Ida Barr? Nothing. . .

ROSE. Your hair blacker than the deep trench my lost twin died in.

JEFF. And so thick, when it was grey it was easy to set.

ROSE. Whose lungs not perforated with tiny millions of holes. Whose voice calls across the silent screen to answer Theda Bara, sing for Lilian Gish.

Both mount platforms, punctuate platform dialogue with buzzes on the foot-buttons.

JEFF. I am an arm.

ROSE. I am a breast. I crush fruit. *(Half orange on breast—breast visible through clothes-flap cut in garment.)*

JEFF. I am an arm and a prayer.

ROSE. Speak my son.

JEFF. Forgive me for the butchered worm. *(Take prick out.)*

ROSE. I am a breast. I feed reptiles. *(Shows breast through flap.)*

JEFF. Forgive me for the child's shit beneath my tongue. *(Eats from suspended piss-pot.)*

ROSE *(shows arse by bending down, dropping knickers).* I am an arse. I milk the summer sky.

JEFF. I am a prayer and a pair of testicles. *(Shows testicles.)*
ROSE. Follicles. Bicycles. I am a complete shithole. *(Farts.)*

Both dismount platforms, move amongst audience.

JEFF. And concerts too, and middle-of-the-yard homecomings. Someone else must supply the piano.
ROSE. I'm a great fat tart, not to be eaten for nothing. A great big pie to be paid for. Lovely dinner fellas–I killed the kid's pet rabbit.
JEFF. She waited for them to finish, then told them. Down they went to the bottom of the garden and there was the cage–empty. Ooh she did laugh.
ROSE. I'm a great big baggage. I'm a breast of tits when one's not bunged in the baby's mouth. I've little hands and delicate feet.
JEFF. Searching for an umbrella to manhandle miscreant children.
ROSE. Deal it out as a down payment for better things. My lovely railway porter who does not have funny legs like the one who led me to the altar.
JEFF. Harry didn't talk to himself like the mad old bugger she had put away. (Only because he had no one to talk to mind.)
ROSE. A bit of the other for you–a bit put by for me. I won't spend my old age doling it out to them that can't get any better.
JEFF. She always kept her dignity, unlike her mate who went on doing it till she was 70. A bit added to the pension from those who can't afford a younger bit.
ROSE. Grab a jeweller second time round, for a tidy little nest egg–but that doesn't stop you shitting yourself when your bowels pack in, doesn't stop you dying in a mess of vomit, doesn't stop the surprise at a hand up your cunt when you want a piss. Doesn't stop a scar like a necklace when the first cancer is taken away. Who'll take my safeguard against the workhouse for a second visit?

Both mount platforms.

JEFF. Forgive me for the war and the state of your mother's transistor set. Bet you love milk or a swift slug of come.
ROSE *(shows breast).* I am a breast. I bleed wool.
JEFF *(touching each).* My leg. My arm. My ankle. My toe.
ROSE. I am a breast. Confess.
JEFF. She jumped aside too slowly for the car to avoid her. Her hips were visibly dislocated from the way she lay in the road. I said 'Do I know you?'
ROSE. I am a buttock. *(Displays one buttock.)*
JEFF. She asked me to go and get help. The driver was dead in a sumptuous lace bouquet of blood. I didn't move. She was in terrible pain. I stood and smiled.

ROSE. I am two buttocks. *(Displays both.)*
JEFF. I stood and smiled as more people came. 'Who is she?' they asked. 'Was she with you?' 'I am alone,' I smiled and asked one of them for a sweet.
ROSE. You may begin your confession.
JEFF. I itch. I feed fleas. Soft bugs ravage me, hooks on their fat faces snapped on my penis.
ROSE. Get to the point.
JEFF. A cloud the size of a hippopotamus has anaesthetised my skull. 'Are you in pain' I inquired politely.
ROSE *(displaying).* I am a belly. Confess.
JEFF. I sit in a belly and the babyshit touching the first pale blue memories of first soap succours my tongue. *(Eats from piss-pot.)* I got in your belly through an angry cunt. Ravaging rags of facemouth churning in grimace mashed me up a toothless channel in hatred hard as a tennis ball.
ROSE *(displaying).* I am a cunt and a successful examination result.
JEFF. Answer me.
ROSE. No.
JEFF. In the nicotine throat I licked the tartar down to a purple paleness. I licked scum till the membrane breathed as pure as pearl. I love your purity.
ROSE. You need my shit.
JEFF. I fly.

Dismount platforms.

JEFF. Ooh she was embarrassed by it. Her with all the airs and graces. Treated like she was better than the others and got to believe it.
ROSE. It's no joke being born in the workhouse.
Carrying around a stigma like that.
The rest of your life may be harder.
JEFF. Considered too good to be brought up with the others so loved elsewhere where her talents might be spotted.
ROSE. But you haven't got that on your birth certificate.
JEFF. Thing is, she didn't know she could change it.
ROSE. Here I am, singing me heart out in quartets in Covent Garden.
JEFF. And pay for the lessons. . .
ROSE. And all the time that in me bureau.
JEFF. She talked like she had a plum in her mouth.
ROSE.
Ai changed me name from Gwendoline.
Ai made it sound refined.
It don't recall the workhouse
And that is most divine.
Ai would have made the front line of course, but me voice is too strong.

Ai would have been a star but me nose is too big. (Drat me mother. shagging what I suspect was a Jew.)
Ai would have been a jewel of musical comedy but ai couldn't see past me false eyelashes. (A thousand curses on me mother for knocking it off with a cross-eyed dipsomaniac.)
Ai could've been the toast of the Talk of the Town, but I slurp me food. (Damn me old lady's sacred bones for doing dirties with a slobbering nincompoop.)
Ai could have been the shining centre of a circle of naice friends if they could stand the smell. (Shit to the old whore for fouling her fanny with a rotting doody, or so I suspect.)
Sod the corpse on the kitchen floor. If the old fart can't get himself a glass of water for his tickly throat without croaking and leaving me a lonely widow. . .

Both mount platforms.

Backgammon. Backslapping. Blackjack. Play with me.
JEFF *(belting tennis ball across space).* My service.
ROSE. Amen. *(Belts one back.)*
JEFF. Ball to you. *(Belts one.)*
ROSE. Eat this. *(Ball.)*
JEFF. Love one. *(Ball.)*
ROSE. Game.
JEFF. Beggar your neighbour. Bugger the other. Suck on the worm fruit. Your deal. *(Ball.)*
ROSE. Five, twenty. Thirty-five, two. Five, twenty, Thirty-five, two. *(Ball.)*
JEFF. And when she started to cry just before the ambulance arrived I took out my own sweets and offered them to all the people. Fifty-two, seventy. *(Ball.)* Game!
ROSE. Scratch me then.
JEFF. It started to rain lightly.
ROSE. Spit on me then.
JEFF. I lifted my face and resisted the ensuing waves of compassion that welled in my body to meet the rain.
ROSE. I am a breast. Drown. Breathe. Good afternoon.

Improvise action.

JEFF. I want to tell you about Sunday. I want to define it.
Sunday is a substance. It is milk.
I want to pin down Sunday. I want to lay the ghost forever. Sunday afternoon is wool and from it matrons make the pullovers of frightened schoolboys with Jesus in their bottoms.
Sunday is grey wool and a roll of flannel. Sunday is a pale boiled pudding, cold but not yet dry. Sunday is the colour of my toes after laying in the bath two hours; the precise white of the severed limb stirring lightly in a bottle. Sunday is a closed shop. All go home.
ROSE. We are both of us close to bankruptcy.
JEFF. I hate you. Buy a paper.

Off the platforms.

JEFF. Course we all felt sorry for the girl, losing her boot in the mud the day the picture was taken, but you couldn't associate yourself with the way she turned out.

ROSE. Now I'm younger. Now I like the sailors in town. Now I get pissed. Now I cross fields, knickers all torn. Straw hat catches a stray edge on a hedge, my hat unwinds. Now I've got a pimple on my head, long stream of pus oozing out behind. Oh mum, what I done! Did I do it?

JEFF. Peered up her twat with a torch to make sure.

ROSE. Me a gay little girl, and won't the fellas pay for one so small.

JEFF. Took a cut for the use of the room. Family economies in these hard times.

ROSE. Now I'm a little older. Grown more, grown inside. How odd not to feed them a special diet, carefully balanced to nurture it. The right amount of bread, of milk, of fruit, of mealworms. How I languish on a hospital bed, a pale angel, my navy blue eyes. If you must give me blood I don't want a Jew's. I've always been generous.

JEFF. She managed to keep her sense of humour.

ROSE. How I age and mature, though I don't look good in daylight and don't often see it. Don't call me Flossy. Call me Molly, it's what I want to be.

JEFF. Gave up one-nighters. She could have made it to the top if she'd had any choice.

ROSE. I dreamed of languishing in a villa in the Swiss Alps, saving the life of little snakes I find in my garden. I'm ready to die. How dull. I smoke less. I smoke just as much, but with filters. I'm all jitters. I talk. I don't talk often. I talk if you come here. I cough. I don't cough so much now. My lip is better. My lip was worth. Thank you for listening. He's away for a worth. While operation. Surgery.

JEFF. She could talk the hind legs off a donkey.

Mount platforms.

ROSE. I remember my breasts. Confess.

JEFF. I saw the golden viper in the flowers behind a rotting gate and I walked past. I ignored it, preferring my dense cloud of insensible indifference. I saw its jewelled back stir in summer, saw the pollen from the labyrinthine hillocks poxed with orchards dust its sticky head.
I walked past, eyes now riveted on tarmac and the cloud that hugged the horizon where the road vanished.

ROSE *(displaying).* I am a cunt and a dozen other possibilities.

JEFF. I saw the viper with his dog-tooth zig-zag, knew his power of breathing roselight into mucus in your bowels. Knew the glister sun gives bright on newcast faeces, flashes knowledge to the dead head, letting colours in with hard prick striking sky.

Off platforms.

Dopey. Like a tit in a trance.
ROSE. Me not destined to be nun and that surprises you.
Me silent and gaze, faintly, abstract, at what?
I pad softly, see my reflections in every place.
Who covered the mirrors as I came in from a hard day?
JEFF. Couldn't take her eyes off herself, a wonder she got anything done.
ROSE. Me, in anger. What to do now to replenish myself. My stare inside, where Arthur weeps to have his eyes put out. Good Hubert do not put out mine eyes. Young sir I must.
JEFF. And how we cried.
ROSE. My stare inside. I hear strains of Claire de Lune, which doesn't end. I suspect benzedrine keeps him awake. I suspect the piano roll has torn before the final movement.
JEFF. He couldn't keep his mind on anything for very long.
ROSE. Me a lost Catholic. Father what shall I do? Don't go to confession I don't do anything wrong. I suspect I'm being got at. Send off a letter at midnight. You can't fool me. I know you're plotting.
JEFF. Called her Annie the Dope.
ROSE. Send off another in the morning to apologise. Which one shall they open first?
I light candles so you'll pass your O Levels.
God's gone and left us to an eneven struddle.
JEFF. Second time round she could have done it in the church according to Father Bannister.

Mounts platforms.

ROSE. I am a head of hair. Sing now.
JEFF. Metal makes a tinny ring and tin makes metal sharper.
ROSE. Gunbarrel.
JEFF. Metal rings a melody that smells of sleeping father.
ROSE. Eiderdown.
JEFF. Metal weighs on blood and bone and makes the eye wax harder.
ROSE. Pokerface.
JEFF. Metal puts my blood to sleep.
ROSE. Nothing.
JEFF. Viper loves me. Viper sings a song of grass and cherries.
ROSE. Teatime.
JEFF. Viper knows snake. Snake knows me and makes my lips less bleary.
ROSE. Spit.
JEFF. Viper wriggles light in whisps of goldgrass at my tearducts.
ROSE. Blubberer.
JEFF. Viper paints me red.

ROSE. Nothing.
JEFF. Sunday sits on celandines and shits on time and sunsets.
ROSE. Dusk.
JEFF. Sunday sits on metal on the leaden weight of tom tits.
ROSE. Twitterbugs.
JEFF. Sunday lies on land, reclines on heavy thoughts of suet.
ROSE. Pudding.
JEFF. Sunday eats you.
ROSE. Nothing.
JEFF. Speak.
ROSE. So I go up to this bloke. . .

Off the platforms.

JEFF. Am I the bloke?
ROSE. You're the bloke.
JEFF. The woman from next door was in attendance.
ROSE. Holding a knitting needle in her hand, trying to keep it still. I attempt some sort of control.
Lying on my back with my knickers off, I try to keep my legs wide apart.
Holding the knitting needle with one hand, keeping my cunt open with the other, I try to steer the needle up on a straight course. I try to keep my nerve. I try to follow instructions.
JEFF. Didn't do it herself. Couldn't lay herself open to prosecution.
ROSE. What lies between me and the knitting needle? What left-overs of love, what dregs of pain? What sweet night among many to startle this growing? What sweet child swelling four months tip-toes on the point of a needle? How many angels can stand on the point of a pin?
JEFF. You've only got yourself to blame, you dirty little whore. I'm not having any more bastards in my house.
ROSE. Who twists and turns exquisitely in torture like a dancer.
JEFF. They all turned out liking culture.
ROSE. Who drags a dead baby round a factory, who plops it to a watery grave down the lavatory with no outward show of ceremony, who feeds the fishes. Who fed on me now feeds me.
I shall not comb my hair. I do not care about my broken tooth.
JEFF. She could have been the best looking if she'd looked after herself.
ROSE. I have a perfect skin. I shall not bother with cream in a hot climate.
JEFF. I used to wear my oldest clothes so I wouldn't make her feel uncomfortable, but I still looked smarter.
ROSE. I shall catch me a genuine man who won't know anything about me.
JEFF. The trouble with marrying an inexperienced man and pretending you don't know anything is that you live forty years with a rotten sex life.

JEFF. I'm the bloke.
ROSE. And I say–
JEFF. What do you say?
ROSE. Wait for it.
JEFF. As long as I'm going to get it.
ROSE. As long as what?
JEFF. Oh, half a yard...
ROSE. No holds barred.
JEFF. What did you say to the man?
ROSE. Fuck me.
JEFF. Just like that.
ROSE. Any way you want.
JEFF. Upstairs or downstairs.
ROSE. In my lady's chamber.
JEFF. In times of stress and danger.
ROSE. All good men must come to the aid of the Party.
JEFF. And what did he say?
ROSE. He ignored me.
JEFF. He ignored you? How?
ROSE. With his ignorance.
JEFF. Was he very ignorant?
ROSE. Just gave an inner grunt.
JEFF. A sort of uggh?
ROSE. Very inner.
JEFF. Dog's dinner.
ROSE. On her and in her.
JEFF. You?
ROSE. No not that day.
JEFF. Let us pray.

Mount platforms.

ROSE. Dearly beloved we are gathered together–
JEFF. A cluster of soft eggs ripe for the fingers.
ROSE. In the sight of God and mankind–
JEFF. Under the celestial telescopic sights.
ROSE. Clinging hand in hand before life's altar–
JEFF. Sweat to sweat. Cheek to cheek.
ROSE. The light from the East window blessing our innocent brows–
JEFF. A thousand gallons of viper piss.
ROSE. Answer our plea we beseech thee . . .
JEFF. Show us the way to Halifax.
ROSE. Show us the route to enlightenment.
JEFF. Where's the fuse box?
ROSE. Ease our sexual pain.
JEFF. Make me Sunday. Make me metal.
ROSE *(lifts flap).* I am a breast.

Off platforms.

JEFF. Old Tommy never minded about the youngest bastard and never knew he was favoured.
ROSE. Not being religious one should choose the best for one's children.
JEFF. Yet it was him that ended up carrying the banner for fertility.
ROSE. Five little Salvationists to transport to Australia.
JEFF. Course one wasn't his own, and he didn't blame Peggy once his own illegitimacy was pointed out to him. And he called the child after his Moral Saviour and made it his favourite.
ROSE. At the wedding of the oldest we sipped orange juice, toasted the bride in lime and didn't smoke.
JEFF. They were queueing up for the toilet.
ROSE. We carried Aston Villa into the Bush.
JEFF. Laughed at their accents when they first went out there.
ROSE. We take the high cheek bones and the King chin to a corner shop in Sydney.
JEFF. He didn't often write to his mother.

Mount platforms.

ROSE. A bucket, a tree, a prickly sensation.
JEFF. The clank of metal sends the geese to flesh around my neck nape. Spring gum peppers concrete under plane trees. Hold my hand.
ROSE. A pepper pot. A chimney pot. Dry rot.
JEFF. Roof to cellar, the fullness and dissemination of my stopcock's squat stature. Cat spray. Seafood. Open the door.
ROSE. My body.
JEFF. I love you with a skin diver's dedication. Salt and sea-weed, rusted U-boats, octotentacles from periscopes. The crust of brine on black nylon.
ROSE. My clothes.
JEFF. I put your soiled garments to my tongue. I draw the salt from stocking soles and perspiration on your collar, moistened, moves with suction. Love your odours. Talcum dusty on the fabric. Pefumes staled from parties past. The smells of men.
ROSE. A motor car.
JEFF. A broad road.
ROSE. Confess.
JEFF. No.
ROSE. I confess an animal I harbour.
I confess a parasite. Food must be found.
Heather Snake? No. Vera Viper? Banished to the halls of sun pollen.
I confess a rat.
JEFF. I am a belly. *(Displays.)*
ROSE. I confess to feeding blood in love to Jack Rat.
Lying with my startled rodent eyes in scuttling empty bedrooms,

Own to feeling forepaws asking me for drink,
Own to pouring personality in wine past pin teeth into anxious throat.
Eyes like my eyes turn in channels where your calm love failed to clear the way. Wounds are cleansing.
Liberal intentions fail the violence of sun in my gut.
Teeth like my teeth ask a yearning death.
I give you a rat.
You give him blood.
Love left is life enough.

JEFF. I am legs, arms and a body.
ROSE. Teacups.

JEFF *(singing).*

Hung on their hooks on the shelf.
Wedgewood and Minton and Delft.
Saucers and plates and cups.
Little flowers, apples and nuts.

Lady Rat sits down to tea
With Rose and Priscilla and me.
Milk first and sugar or lemon
And blood with a creaming of semen.

The afternoon streams through the chintz
Priscilla's the palest of tints
While Rose is the Rosiest hue
And Lady Rat knows what to do.

The pale child of life is fed death.
The funeral Rose fouled her breath
And Lady Rat stirs in her fat
And that is the outcome of that.

Off platforms.

ROSE. How many to join the tattered ghosts, the hollow old man of forty-nine mumbling to himself and spitting blood, the flabby old lady, her lymph system transferring cancer spores to every inch. Wrinkled yellow potatoes clasp the hands of idiot children. Dorothy, May and Billy died of meningitis and don't tell me that's not to do with the brain.
There's a bloated drowned corpse that tries to walk erect like a sailor should, who stumbles trying to assemble bomb-shattered limbs.
They mutter hail Marys.

Mount platforms.

ROSE. I've got a stomach ache.
JEFF. Cocoa.

ROSE. I've got a hole.
JEFF. Crumpet.
ROSE. I've a gash in my side and vaginas in my palms.
JEFF. That's handy.
ROSE. I want you to hear the wind at my side. I wish you could catch the soughing chord.
I wish you could hear the song of lack
And the hard need moaning through cold veins.
I want no vault of void to cleave to.
I choose no bottomless cellar to need.
I want you to have the love I reserve for my unwanted dying, to warm the air,
The love I retain in my blood for the cold breath of nothing.
The warmth for my cuts I'd give you if I could.
JEFF. Iodine.